Frank Sargeant's

Secret Spots

Southwest Florida

Florida's Best Saltwater Fishing From Sarasota Bay to Marco

by Frank Sargeant

A LARSEN'S OUTDOOR PUBLISHING BOOK
THE ROWMAN & LITTLEFIELD PUBLISHING GROUP, INC.
Lanham • Chicago • New York • Toronto • Plymouth, UK

Published by
LARSEN'S OUTDOOR PUBLISHING
An imprint of The Rowman & Littlefield Publishing Group, Inc.
4501 Forbes Boulevard, Suite 200, Lanham, Maryland 20706
http://www.rlpgtrade.com

Estover Road, Plymouth PL6 7PY, United Kingdom

Distributed by National Book Network

British Library Cataloguing in Publication Information Available

Library of Congress Cataloging-in-Publication Data Available

Library of Congress 93-79802

ISBN:978-0-936513-36-2 (paper : alk.paper)

♾™ The paper used in this publication meets the minimum
requirements of American National Standard for Information
Sciences—Permanence of Paper for Printed Library Materials,
ANSI/NISO Z39.48-1992.

Printed in the United States of America

DEDICATION

This book is dedicated to my sons Brock and Brian, and to my wife Darla, who have put up with my 4 a.m. risings, my muddy feet and my tangles of tackle for many years, usually without complaint.

PREFACE

Catching fish is not tough, if you know where to look.

But knowing where to look separates the men from the boys-- or the snook from the snookers, as the case may be.

This book can go a long way toward helping you know where to look. It's based on more than 25 years of fishing Florida's inshore waters personally, and on the observations of dozens of good friends, many of them professional guides, who have been kind enough to assist and share a few of their secrets.

SECRET SPOTS, Sarasota Bay to Marco, covers my personal favorite region of all the waters in Florida, the southwest coast. No where else has the variety and the abundance of fine inshore gamefish, plus the huge acreage of clear, shallow grass flats.

Just remember, as you use this book to explore these waters, that those grass flats are what create the excellent fishing, and they are fragile. As more and more boats begin to fish these waters, the grass is more and more vulnerable. Do your part to avoid damaging it by knowing the draft of your hull and prop, and never running in water so shallow that you uproot this delicate and essential part of the ecosystem.

• •

Another word of caution. Many secret spots remain secret because they're tough to find or tough to get to. This book contains many inshore spots that are risky or downright dangerous to approach if you're not familiar with shallow water operation.

Go slowly, go cautiously, and keep your eyes open anytime you approach an inshore location. Unmarked rocks, bars, pilings and other hazards are part of the flats fishing game, and running at speed in waters you don't know can wipe out your lower unit or even hole your boat in extreme cases. Discretion is definitely the better part of valor in running the inside waters.

Remember, too, that the National Oceanic and Atmospheric Administration Nautical Charts on which the maps are based have in some cases not been updated for 10 years or more. While most areas along the west coast do not see dramatic changes in bottom structure, depths in passes and over bars can alter enough in a matter of days to put you aground. Let your depth finder and your own eyes be the ultimate judge of safe depths, using the charts only as a general guide.

Contents

HOW TO USE THE CHARTS

The charts in this book are based on the offical U.S. government charts produced by the National Ocean Survey. However, because the charts have been sectioned to fit the format of the pages, not all navigation markers and hazards to navigation are shown. And, some charts have been reduced in scale, others expanded, which changes the apparent distances between markers and obstructions.

DO NOT DEPEND ON THE CHARTS IN THIS BOOK FOR SAFE NAVIGATION!

They are offered only as a guide to good fishing spots. Remember, too, that some of the areas shown as holding fish will be fishable by boat only on high tide--and may be completely dry on some low tides!

Key your use of the charts to the seasons. While trout, redfish, snapper and snook are shown well inland in some of the rivers, remember that these locations will produce only in winter, when the fish move inshore to find warmer water. Conversely, species like tarpon and mackerel, shown at the outer edge of the grass flats, will be found there only in temperate weather, spring through fall.

Similarly, areas on the flats showing snook, trout, flounder and reds are likely to produce best on rising or high tides, while swash channels, creek mouths and dredge holes are better bets on low or falling tides.

Adjust your fishing to the seasons, tides and weather conditions, and try a series of the indicated spots until you find action. Remember, no ''secret spot'' produces every time, but by selecting your spot based on prevailing conditions, you'll frequently find action.

LIST OF CHARTS

(cont'd)

LIST OF CHARTS *(cont'd)*

About The Author

Frank Sargeant is outdoors editor of the Tampa Tribune and a senior writer for Southern Outdoors and BassMaster magazines. he was formerly an editor for CBS Publications, and a writer for Disney World Publications, as well as southern editor for Outdoor Life. His writing and photos have appeared in a wide variety of other publications, including Field & Stream, Sports Afield,

 Popular Mechanics, Popular Science and The Reader's Digest. He was a fishing guide before becoming a writer and editor.

He holds a masters degree in English and Creative Writing from Ohio University and has taught writing at the high school and college level. Sargeant's works have won more than 40 national awards in the past decade. he is also author of the best-selling Inshore Library: THE SNOOK BOOK, THE REDFISH BOOK, THE TARPON BOOK and THE TROUT BOOK, as well as the first in this regional Saltwater Series: Frank Sargeant's Secret Spots - Tampa Bay to Cedar Key.

Further information on these books is available in the Resource Directory at the back of the book. Sargeant lives on the Little Manatee River near Tampa, Florida.

CHAPTER 1

SARASOTA BAY

Ten miles long and three miles wide, Sarasota Bay is a respectable piece of water--but it doesn't get much respect. Aced on the south by Charlotte Harbor and on the north by Tampa Bay, Sarasota is a card rarely played by traveling anglers, but it's highly productive for those who know how and where to fish it.

The bay gets an abundant flow of gulf water through three passes, with Longboat Pass on the north end, New Pass about four-fifths of the length southward, and Big Sarasota Pass on the south end. The swank developments of Longboat Key form much of the western shore of the bay, while the Sarasota/Bradenton metro area walls much of the eastern shore.

Yet, despite the development and some pollution problems, the continual flushing of tidal waters keep the bay in relatively good condition, and the usually-abundant bait supply assures plenty of gamefish. The bay is also in the process of being protected under the National Estuaries Program, so the future looks bright.

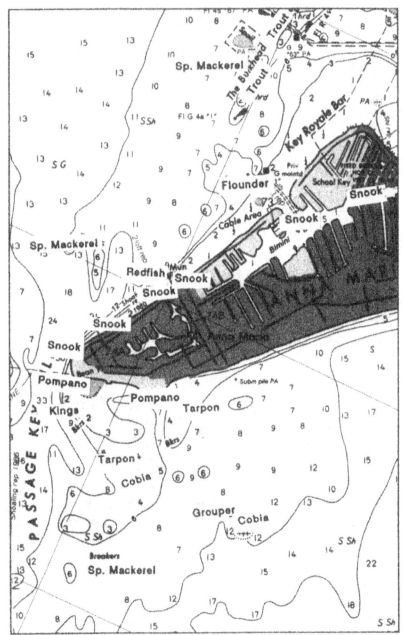

Passage Key Inlet to The Bulkhead

Captain Jim O'Neill shows a redfish taken in Palma Sola Bay. Weedless gold spoons do the job here.

PALMA SOLA BAY

This small bay is a good windy-day hideaway, and often has good trout fishing in winter. I was fishing a 2-foot-deep flat near the entrance channel with Captain Jim O'Neill one fall afternoon when what seemed to be the whole bottom rose up and began to swim away from us. It was a monster school of redfish, so many they turned the water copper in the afternoon sun. Our spoons didn't move a foot before we were both connected to robust 6-pounders. Next cast, same result, and so on until the fish pushed off the flat. A little later on we flipped live sardines into the 9-foot channel, and O'Neill decked a keeper-size gag grouper while I was reeling in a snook. The bay is only about a mile across, but because it offers such a variety of habitat, it's a dependable producer.

SARASOTA BAY NORTH

The north end of the bay, extending from the Cortez Bridge to Whale Key Bar, is mostly shallow and has lots of grassy bottom that's attractive to trout. Average depth here is 1 to 2 feet on broad shoals that extend as much as a half-mile from shore in many areas, with 4 to 6 feet in the channels.

Karl Wickstrom, publisher of Florida Sportsman Magazine, shows a whopper trout taken on Zara Spook near Whale Cay Bar with Captain Johnny Walker.

On the flats, there are numerous sand holes, and the now-famed live sardine methods first made popular by Captain Scott Moore (who grew up in Bradenton Beach) are deadly here.

(For those unfamiliar--you cast-net the sardines, which can be chummed into range on the edge of the grass flats nearest the passes with a mix of whole wheat bread, canned sardines and canned jack mackerel. The baits are then used as live chum themselves, pitched over the holes, and are also free-lined on 1/0 hooks and light spinning gear to draw the strikes. It's devastating for all three of the primary flats species.)

Though we know that development, seawalling and mangrove destruction is very detrimental to overall productivity of any estuary, fish are adaptable creatures, and those that make Sarasota Bay their home have learned to thrive in the artificial environment. The spoil islands that have been dug up to create the boat channels now attract mullet and crabs, and reds and trout frequently prowl the tips of these islands. The canals that lead to the million-dollar-homes are all deep-water refuges for snook and trout in winter, and the channels leading across the flats to

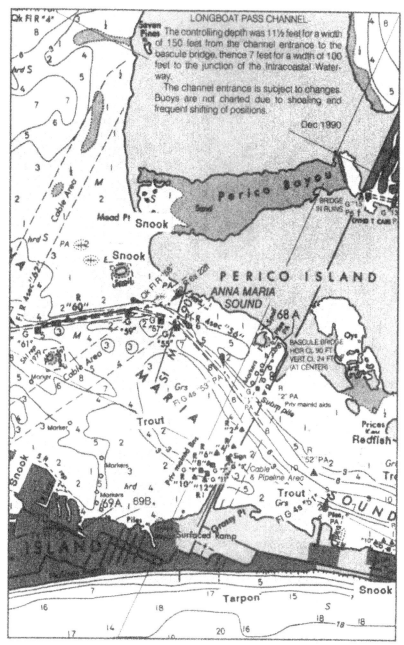

ANNA MARIA SOUND

By casting a swimming jig up on the shoal and swimming it down just above the grass in 3 to 5 feet of water, you'll find lots of trout in fall and winter.

these spots often hold flounder, reds, and a bit of everything else on spring low tides year around.

The Whale Key Bar itself is a prime spot for big trout in spring, and for schoolers in fall. It extends roughly a mile eastward from Whale Key, and lies south of ICW markers 18 to 21. The surrounding water is about 8 feet deep, but the bar is anywhere from 1 to 3 feet deep, a great place to throw topwaters at dawn and dusk on moving tides.

CORTEZ

Though the marinas south of the Cortez Bridge are home of the alleged "bad guys" of many of Florida's coastal fishery problems, the numerous net boats in this area don't seem to do a lot of harm to the fishery--or at least the fishery remains pretty good in spite of them. There are many holes and points within shouting distance of the marinas that frequently hold trout from October through May, and snook from March through November. Particularly where the holes are found between islands or on points where tide flow is strongest, the fish dependably gather.

Another good pattern in this area is to fish the deep grass where the flats fall off into the main channel. These grassy areas are not broad, most not spanning a hundred yards, but they run

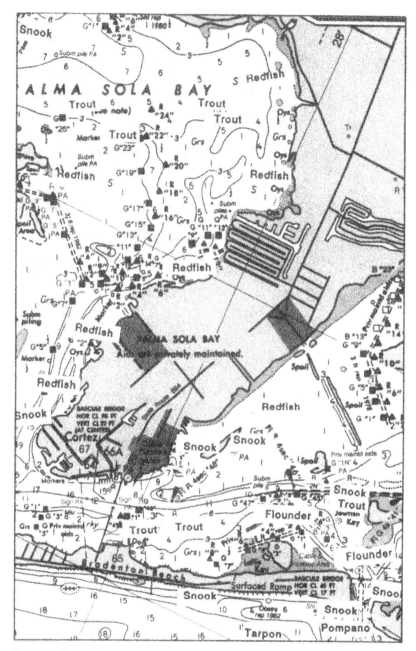

PALMA SOLA BAY

21

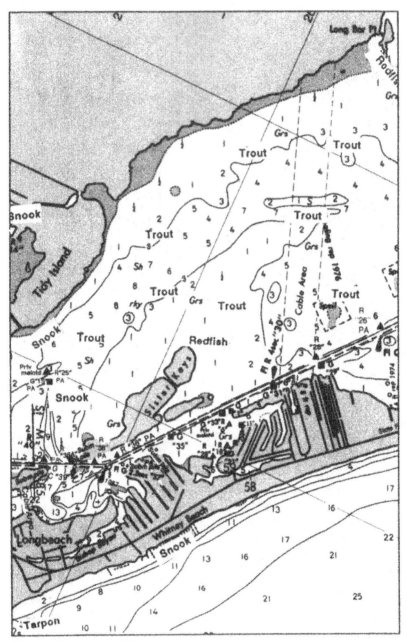

NORTH SARASOTA BAY

22

parallel to the channel for long distances. By casting a Rattlin' Flash, 52-M Mirr-O-Lure or a swimming jig up on the shoal and swimming it down just above the grass in 3 to 5 feet of water, you'll find lots of trout in fall and winter. Work the jig more slowly and you'll catch big flounder in the same area. And work up on the edges in early fall and you'll often find cruising redfish. The action is often particularly good between the Cortez Bridge and Leffis Key.

Also check out the grass pockets between the spoil bars, which are just east of the ICW markers. Working through this area on the push pole will turn up redfish and nice trout in October and November, and again in spring.

LONGBOAT PASS

The waters around Longboat Pass offer a potpourri of inshore and beach species. On the outside bar, you're very likely to spot cruising tarpon from late April through June. Most anglers motor-fish these schools, which works ok when they first arrive, but spooks them later. Using a couple of electric trolling motors to get within casting range is a better approach. Live crabs are the can't-fail bait, but sardines, pinfish and finger-mullet are also good. And they'll sometimes take sinking plugs or 5/0 streamer flies.

Longboat also holds some very large snook in summer, though this is not a famed snooking pass like some further south. The north bar is a good place to cast the surf after sundown with a big Long A Bomber, and the inside basin is also worth checking from June through September. Deepest water here is not in the main pass, but on the dogleg to the south, where there's as much as 22 feet in close to the docks--good spots to probe with live shrimp after dark.

THE MAIN BAY

Sarasota Bay proper is a bowl averaging about 10 feet deep, with few bars away from the shorelines. Because the bottom is relatively flat and featureless, it's not generally great fishing.

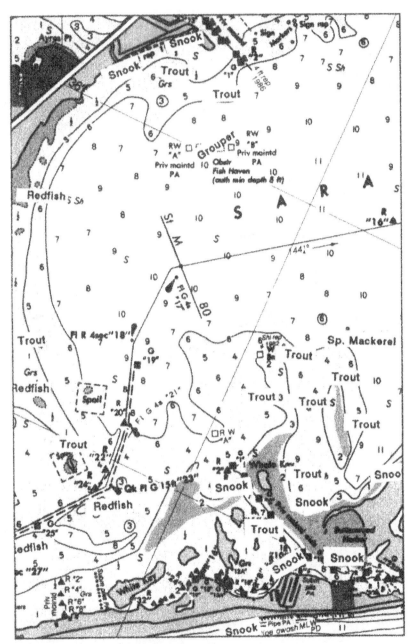

WHALE KEY BAR IN SARASOTA BAY

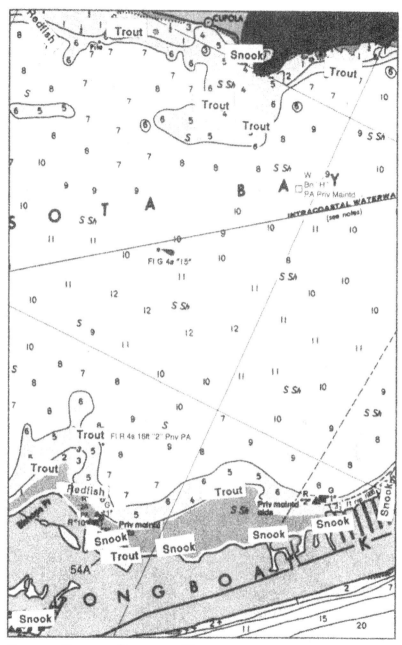

BISHOPS POINT IN SARASOTA BAY

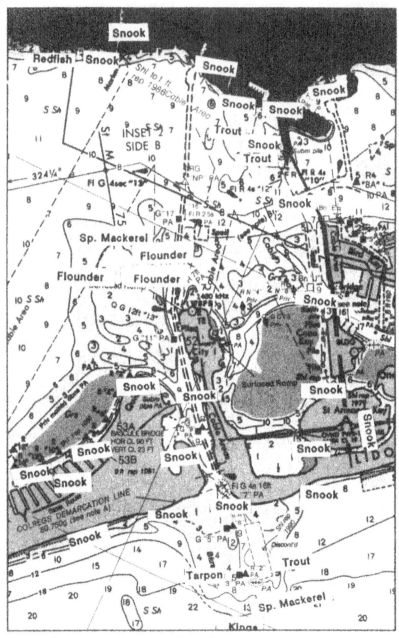

SOUTH SARASOTA BAY AND NEW PASS

However, when glass minnows swarm in through the passes in fall, large schools of trout, ladyfish, jacks and a few Spanish often come with them, and if you get on one of these pods--which you can locate by watching for diving gulls--you can wear yourself out landing fish. Small gold or silver jigs are the ticket. You'll sometimes find even bluefish mixed with the trout.

The eastern shore has several broad, grassy flats where trout are usually abundant, with the one in front of the Ringling Museum noted as particularly productive. Local experts like Captain Johnny Walker fish live pigfish in spring and take some whopper trout in this area.

Some of the cuts that lead to marinas on the Longboat side have deep dredgeholes in them, and historically these spots produced heavy catches of monster trout 6 to 8 pounds. It's rare to get one that big these days, but the holes still collect good numbers of smaller trout on cold days in December.

NEW PASS

New Pass is a killer area for snook pretty much year around. Tremendous numbers gather there from late May through August to spawn, and the rest of the year the fish hang around the docks and the bridge to feed. There's a deep boat basin on the north side where fish often pod up around the boats and along the mangrove shoreline during the spawn, and they're also found along the length of City Island and in the dogleg that makes off to the north around Longboat. On falling tides, the slough near the beach on the south side of the inlet can be good, especially after dark.

The middle bridge leading to St. Armands Key from Sarasota has as much as 17 feet of water underneath, and holds some torpedo-size snook pretty much year around.

BIG SARASOTA PASS

This is a jumbo-sized pass, with jumbo-sized fish to match. It's broad and it's deep, with some areas exceeding 25 feet, lots of water over 15 feet. The pass naturally holds lots of big snook, particularly along the south shore where there's lots of riprap

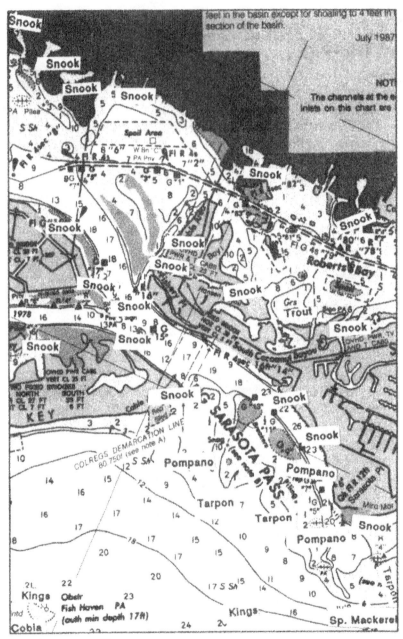

BIG SARASOTA PASS

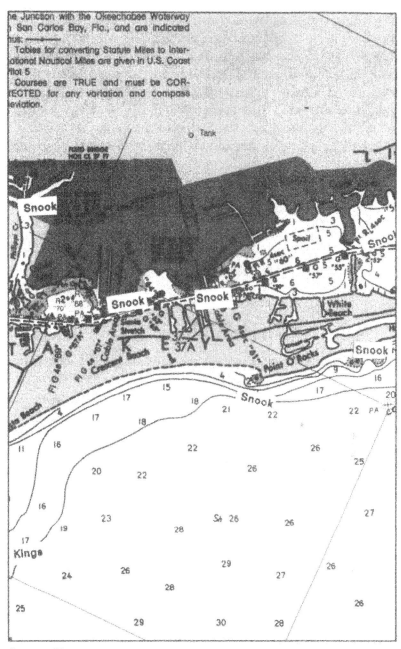

Siesta Key

and steep channel edges, and drifting these edges with a live pigfish trailed just off bottom will connect you with some tackle-busters. You're also likely to find yourself looking over your head at a 6-foot tarpon in this area in late summer. Tarpon also hang around outside the bar in good numbers, and there are Spanish in the same area spring and fall, with kings a little beyond the Spanish when the baitfish schools are in close. If you're interested in a pompano or three for the table, you can bounce a little jig along the bar or on the beach at the pass, or fish bottom with a sand flea in spring. The area is a noted producer of this delicious fish in commercial quantities.

The back side of Roberts Bay, to the south, has several dredged boat basins that often hold nice snook and reds, and in winter trout. There are numerous grassy points and spoil bars on the west side of Roberts that are worth casting a topwater early on spring mornings for trophy-sized trout and the occasional redfish or snook.

LITTLE SARASOTA BAY

Little Sarasota Bay is more just a wide spot in the ICW than a true bay, but because it has been channeled over the years by passes that open and then close at the whim of gulf storms, it's a productive fishery. Midnight Pass is pretty much shoaled shut most of the time, but there are deep channels on the inside where snook and trout like to hang out. One of these passes north inside Bird Key, with numerous bars at the edge of the 9-foot channel. Fish the edge on falling water, and up on the bars and the adjacent flats on the rise.

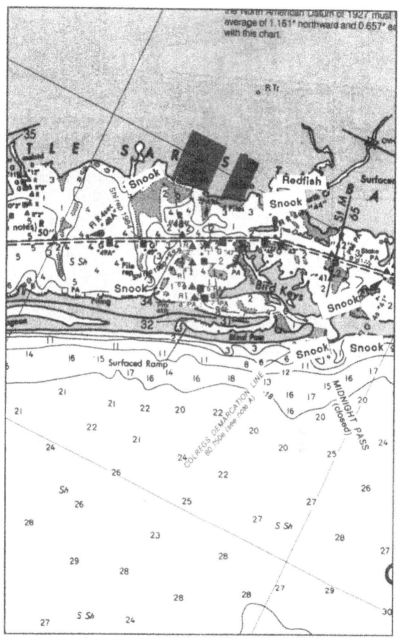

LITTLE SARASOTA BAY

CHAPTER 2

LITTLE RIVERS, BIG SNOOK

Snook up to 30 pounds invade coastal rivers along southwest Florida when the waters on the inshore flats turns chilly, and from early November through the end of December, provide spectacular light-tackle action.

The northern limit is Tarpon Springs and the Anclote River, also just about the northern limit of the snook's range in U.S. waters, though some strays are occasionally found further up the coast in summer. From the Anclote southward, good winter snook rivers include the Pithlachascotee, Hillsborough, Palm, Alafia, Little Manatee, Manatee, Braden, Myakka, Peace and Caloosahatchee. All the creeks and rivers of the Everglades are also prime in winter.

The great thing about snook in these blackwater rivers in winter is that they are strongly inclined to attack topwater plugs, much more so than when they're on the clear flats in summer. Apparently the lower visibility, combined with the lower food availability, makes the linesiders more susceptible to being fooled by the floaters.

The best fishing for big fish is usually in November, before the "keepers" of 24 inches and up get picked over. It's no longer a secret that snook go in the rivers with the first fronts of winter, and plenty of anglers show up as often as they can skip work to take their daily two-some. Thus, by the end of December, you may be catching only undersized fish on some waters because most of the larger fish have been harvested, or at least taught to be somewhat distrustful when a Zara Spook comes burbling overhead.

The fishing remains good despite the unpredictable winter weather. The wind won't hurt you up the rivers, no matter how hard it blows, and unless it gets below freezing, the fish keep right on biting through the winter.

There are a few cautions, to be sure. If you move upstream of the normal navigation markers, the waters may be shallow between the deep snook holes. Some of these rivers have limerock bottoms as you go into the brackish areas, and there are numerous unmarked shoals. Caution and low speed are essential on your first trips into many flowages.

HOW DO YOU FIND THE BEST SPOTS?

In general, seek water deeper than 8 feet, and areas with a strong current flow. The fish are up the rivers looking for warmth, and depth means warmth when a freezing front blows through. The strong flows are natural spots for snook to settle, winter or summer.

Until you find your own secret honey holes, best way to locate these winter fish is to work upstream on an electric trolling motor on a bass boat or flats rig, casting the shoreline, bars and points anywhere the water is deeper than 4 feet. (Go on an incoming tide and you'll find it a lot easier to keep up the pace with the electric motor.)

Jigs, slow-sinking plugs and live shrimp all work well in the rivers, but topwaters are so effective and so much fun that there's not much reason to try anything else most days--if the fish are there, they'll usually belt the floater.

In winter, snook move into coastal rivers and creeks, which are considerably warmer than the surrounding flats. Action usually begins in early November and peaks between Thanksgiving and Christmas. The fish readily take topwaters.

Some of the better lures include the Bangolure SP-5, the MirrOlure 5M, 7M and 28M, and the Bomber Long A. If the fish are running small, you can't beat a size 13 Rapala, though the small hooks on this lure make it suspect for big fish. If you're willing to wait for a big one, a Magnum Rapala or a Zara Spook are the ticket.

All of these are worked with short, sharp snaps of the rod tip, enough to make them dart and flash but not enough to make them move very far across the surface. If you give a bit of slack after each flick of the rod tip, the lure will do about what the fish want. Use the reel only to take up slack, not to move the lure--that's all done with rod action. When the lure gives off a loud "schlurp" every now and then, you've got the action right.

(Anglers handy with a 10-weight flyrod will also find the river fish ready to take 1/0 "slider" type poppers in yellow or white. Tail dressing should be about three inches long. You might want to overload the rod with floating 12-weight WF line, since casts will be short in many areas, with little line out the tip to flex the rod.)

Sometimes it is necessary to follow up a topwater with a jig to draw the hit.

All the lures are fished on 18 inches of 25-pound-test monofilament shock leader to prevent cutoffs on the sharp gill-plates of the fish. Most anglers tie on their lures with a loop knot, and tie the leader to the running line with a double Uni or a blood knot. Use of snaps and swivels seem to reduce the number of strikes on topwaters.

Standard bass tackle, a revolving spool baitcaster with 12- to 15-pound-test mono and a two-hand rod about 6 1/2 feet long is the ideal rig. It doesn't have to be a rug-beater, but it should have a stout base to allow you to muscle the fish away from the mangroves if necessary. (Don't overlook the new braided lines

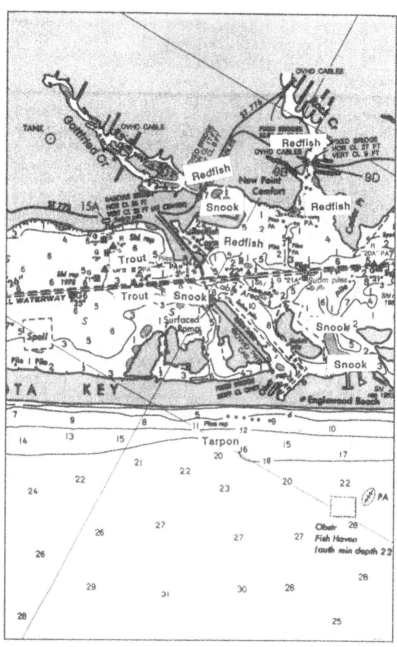

ENGLEWOOD BEACH

recently on the market. Their low stretch and maximum power make them perfect for backwater snook. They seem to backlash less than mono, and wear longer, as well, though they're very expensive.)

The fish feed on the tide flows, working up into the small creeks, around the bars and under the mangrove roots on the rise, and falling back to creek and canal mouths and the deeper channels on the fall. Best fishing is usually on the fall, because the dropping water pulls a lot of minnows and crabs out with it, inspiring the snook to feed.

The fish are usually found in pods, and it's not uncommon to catch a half-dozen from one creek mouth. They frequently swirl at the plugs without taking, but often grab the next toss to the same spot. At times, it may be necessary to follow up the topwater with a jig to draw the hit. Anglers who know the water and the tides routinely pull into particular cuts on a particular flow, drop the anchor and wear them out for 30 minutes or so before the peak at that spot ends.

Interestingly, in some rivers the fish go all the way up to water that's completely fresh, and you'll sometimes catch a snook on one cast and a largemouth bass on the next. Fish have been known to move inland as far as Wauchula on the Peace River, at which point they're some 40 miles from Charlotte Harbor. The greatest numbers are usually closer to the saltwater than this, within 2 to 7 miles of the mouth, but snook can do surprisingly well in fresh water. (In fact, a friend of mine kept three of them alive in a freshwater pond for three years. They grew from five-pounders to 10-pounders in that time, on a diet of bluegills, before finally succumbing to a January freeze.)

The action continues into late March most years, with the fish gradually working their way down the rivers as the water warms--and sometimes hurrying back inland if a late cold front comes through. By the time the water hits 70 degrees on the flats, the fish will all be outside again, but until then, you can catch some awfully big snook in some awfully small Florida rivers.

CHAPTER 3

TARPON ON THE BEACH

It may be Florida's best tarpon fishing, and it's almost unknown.

The west coast beaches from Tampa Bay to Marco Island hold an incredible concentration of fish from early May to mid-July. Yet on most weekday mornings, it's rare to sight another boat as you cast your plug or live bait at seemingly unlimited schools of passing fish.

A trip I made with Captain Kenny Shannon out of Venice Inlet, 60 miles south of Tampa, was typical. We left a public ramp just inside the inlet at first light, motored a few miles up the beach and spotted our first school as the sun began to rise.

"They're at 2 o'clock, a pod of 80-pounders," Shannon advised as he hit the switch on his twin 24-volt trolling motors. The Mako 17 scooted to intersect the path of travel of the rapidly-moving fish, their broad, silver green backs glinting in the early light. We were no more than 200 yards off the white sand beach.

When we were 30 yards away, both of us fired live blue crabs in their direction, throwing ahead of and beyond the school.

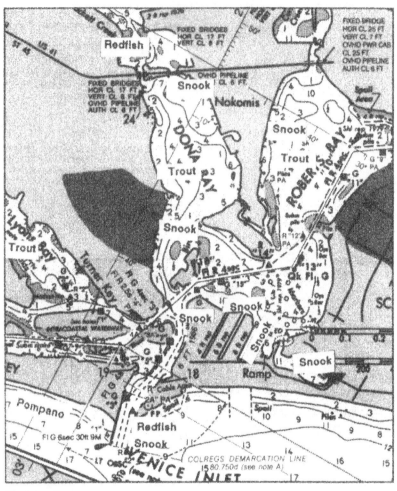

VENICE INLET

Buck fever time as the horse-like fish rolled toward the baits, gulping air through bucket-sized mouths.

My crab sank out of sight in the green water. I took up the bow of slack on the big spinning reel, scooting him directly into their path.

The line bounced, then straightened. I let the fish draw the rod tip down, then slapped the big 7/0 home with four quick jabs of the stout, 7-foot rod.

He instantly started doing those crazy tarpon things. The 5-foot missile launched straight into the rising sun, exploded back into the Gulf, swapped ends, grayhounded twice, did a tail-standing head shake that rattled his gills, and then tore off 150 yards of line as the drag on the big Penn howled.

"We're having fun now," Shannon grinned, easing after the fish on the trolling motor.

Fifteen minutes later the fish yielded to the insistent pressure of the 25-pound-test mono and gasped at boatside. Shannon used a lip-gaff to hold him for pictures and tagging, then eased him back to swim away.

Shannon didn't bother to start the engine.

"There's another pod coming right at us," he said, pointing out the distant fish.

Ten minutes later, we were fast to another tarpon.

And so it went throughout that long June morning. There was rarely 15 minutes when we were not within sight of fish or hooked up.

Shannon said his best days have produced as high as 19 hook-ups from dawn until noon. The average catch for the few guides who concentrate on the run is two fish brought to the boat daily, six to eight hooked.

It's remarkable fishing, and yet none but a few locals regularly enjoy it. This is particularly ironic considering that Boca Grande Pass, the world's best-known and hardest-fished tarpon spot, sits smack in the middle of this stretch of beach. While boats literally bump rubrails to get at the fish in the big pass, the thousands of silver kings that roam the beaches are largely ignored.

The fish are found in water from 10 to 25 feet deep, usually from 200 to 500 yards off the beach--they're thus accessible to boats of all sizes. They tend to travel parallel to the beach,

Tarpon like this one taken by Captain Kenny Shannon near Venice are abundant along the Gulf beaches from May through mid-July. Live blue crabs are the unbeatable bait, but the fish also take sinking plugs and streamer flies.

moving steadily except for occasional stops to feed or "daisy chain".

Fish are particularly likely to show around the bars that make up around each of the passes along the southwest coast. Each of the bars at the mouths of Tampa Bay's three channels produces, with particularly good areas at Passage Key and Bean Point. The mile-long shoal north of Longboat Pass is always a good spot to check, as are the extensive bars around Big Sarasota Pass.

Stump Pass, at the mouth of Lemon Bay, is often good. Both the north and south shoals at Gasparilla Pass are frequently productive. And in recent springs, anglers at Johnson Shoal, just south of the famed tarpon-gathering spot at Boca Grande, have been sighting up to a thousand fish a day!

The long bars at Captiva Pass and Redfish Pass are also likely locations, as is the huge bar off Point Ybel, on the south end of Sanibel Island. San Carlos Bay also has extensive shoals surrounding it, likely areas to check for tarpon that move in off the feeding grounds a bit further out. There's also great fishing within sight of Fort Myers Beach, and around the mouths of the small inlets to the south.

Big Marco Pass, at the north end of Marco, and Cape Romano, at the south end, both have extensive shoals where tarpon frequently congregate.

In each of these locations, the procedure is similar. Since the shoals are small and the water is clear, a slow, silent approach is required--guides usually shut down several hundred yards away and let the wind and tide put them within range.

Shannon and other guides use live blue crabs because the baits are durable, easy to cast and much-loved by the tarpon, but mullet, pinfish, sardines and other small baits are equally acceptable. The fish also readily take sinking plugs such as the Bagley Finger Mullet and the 65M-MirrOlure, and can occasionally be caught on flies, though the deep water makes it tough to get the streamer down to their level.

The fishing is so dependable that Shannon once went 47 days in a row without a miss, tagging at least one fish daily and sometimes up to 10.

The fish are big, but not the giants found further north at the Homosassa flats. Most run between 50 and 80 pounds, though occasionally a monster female in the 150-pound-class crashes the show.

Most anglers use medium spinning tackle, which allows the tarpon to strut their stuff, but when handled right has the authority to bring the average fish to the boat in under 20 minutes. This is good both for the angler and the fish, and makes it more certain that the tarpon will swim off to fight another day. Baitcasters are also good in experienced hands, provided the reel holds at least 250 yards of line. For fly-rodding, the usual 12-weight tackle with Scientific Anglers Mono-core ''slime-line'' is the ticket.

The action is best in the morning, when the sea is usually calm at this time of year. Shortly after noon, a westerly sea breeze springs up, making the water bumpy and also making it harder to see approaching fish.

The trick to getting bit consistently is to spot the fish at long range, run the boat around them in a broad circle that keeps you

Heavy-duty spinning gear makes it easy to present an unweighted live bait to the fish. Most anglers use 25-pound-test on spinning gear. Medium baitcasters with 25- to 30-pound-test are also effective.

at least 300 yards away, and then shut down the outboard and let them swim into range as you make final adjustments with an electric trolling motor.

The reason most amateurs have problems with beach fish is that they attempt to motor directly into casting range, which inevitably puts the fish down.

Presentation is also a bit tricky. If you throw a slow-sinking bait such as a crab directly in front of rolling fish, chances are that they'll pass under it without ever noticing. The successful cast lands about 50 feet ahead of the school, and has sunk down 6 to 10 feet by the time they arrive. There are usually lots of fish below and behind the leaders you see rolling on top, and these hidden fish are the ones that take most of the time.

Most guides use about 5 feet of 100-pound-test leader, tied to just enough double line to allow making a good line-leader connection. This rigging creates minimal casting problems, and gives the gaff man a "handle" to draw the tarpon in close for de-hooking.

HOOKING TARPON

Shannon and some other guides are now using a unique hook produced by the Owner Corporation, known as the "Gorilla Big Game" version. It's aptly named, a forged monster of a hook that's about twice as thick as a normal saltwater hook, but has a razor edged shovel-point. The hook looks a bit like the circle hooks used by long-line fishermen, and has an uncanny ability to stay put in a tarpon's hard mouth.

Tarpon are among the toughest of all fish to hook, no doubt about it. But with the right hook and the right techniques, you can win the game 90 percent of the time.

First, of course, the hooks must be razor-sharp, the line must be strong enough to stretch little at the set, and the rod must have all the whip of a shovel handle.

But just as importantly, according to Captain Kenny Shannon, is letting the fish help you set the hook.

"If you throw to fish coming straight at you, you're going to have a very tough time setting the hook because they keep right on moving as they eat the bait," he notes. "When you set, you've got instant slack, and you're pulling straight away from the fish-- your chance of landing that fish is about zero."

Much better, he notes, is to make the presentation from the side, or when throwing live baits, even from slightly behind. You cast ahead of the fish and let them take going away. (This won't work with artificials, because tarpon never take a lure that seems to be "attacking" them.)

"In this situation, the fish is taking the slack out of your line for you, and the set will pull the hook into the upper corner of his jaw 95 percent of the time," he says.

The beach action stays good until about July 15 most years, at which time the fish pack up and head offshore, apparently to spawn at the edge of the continental shelf. Where they go from there is anybody's guess, but it's for sure that they'll return to the beaches again come spring.

CHAPTER 4

GASPARILLA SOUND

Many anglers view Gasparilla Sound as nothing more than the highway to Charlotte Harbor, rather than as a fishery in its own right. That can be a mistake, because often you run right past a lot more fish than you're going to find after that frequently-bumpy ride south.

Launching areas for the sound are all near Placida. Blessedly, there's now a new, free boat ramp on the Gasparilla Causeway, just before you get to Eldred's. Don't expect to use it if you arrive after daybreak on weekends, because parking is limited, but on weekdays it's a break. Otherwise, you pay to launch here, either on the worn ramp at Eldred's or at the much smoother but more expensive cement ramp at Gasparilla Marine, just south of the Causeway. You can also launch on Gasparilla Island itself and save the run down Gasparilla Sound, but that's very expensive, $5.20 (towing a boat) for the bridge toll plus another $10 to $12 to use available ramps on the island--they don't make allowances for fishermen on this hideaway of millionaires.

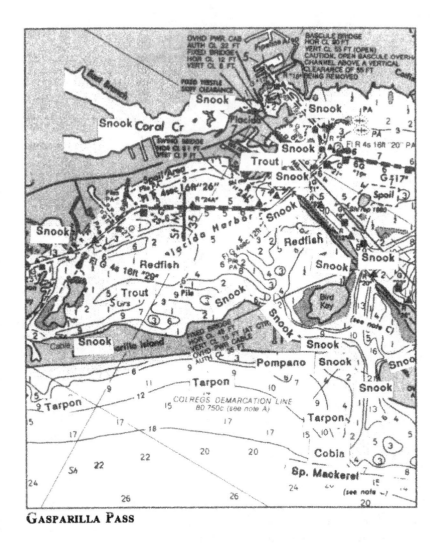

GASPARILLA PASS

PLACIDA

Incidentally, if you've ever wondered about the fenced compound on the south side of the Boca Grande Causeway--that's the Mercury Marine test center, where they put thousands of hours on the Mercs of the future, running them day and night on test beds until something breaks. They also run a fleet of test boats out of the center, identifiable by their bright yellow color. You'll see the boats roaring up and down Gasparilla Sound regularly. The entry channel to the center is a good spot to catch some big trout in winter, but don't get beyond the first buildings or somebody will come out and scold you--they have a lot of secret stuff in there and can't allow the public inside. Also of interest is the mouth of the channel on the south side of this complex, which is where they run their test bed. The tremendous water flow generated by the motors boils the water constantly, which usually attracts bait, which sometimes attracts trout, snook or reds. Here again, you have to confine your fishing to the outer end of the channel to avoid attracting the interest of Merc security.

CATFISH CREEK

The channel into Gasparilla Marine is dredged to 7 feet, and in winter it's a part of the fish-highway into Catfish Creek, which winds off to the north and east. You'll catch some big trout here in late November and through December, as well as snook on occasion. The trout are best caught on 1/4 ounce jigs tapped along bottom, while the snook like topwaters.

As you head south along this shoreline, there are abundant oyster bars within a hundred yards of the mangroves--bad for your lower unit, good for redfish and snook. Most of these bars come out of the water on low tide, but are awash on high--which is the best time to fish them. Those around Catfish Point can be particularly productive on the first part of a falling tide, as the water comes pouring out of Catfish Creek, bringing lots of bait with it. The "narrows" up inside the creek, where oyster bars and mangrove islands restrict the flow, can also be good on the fall, but the water is very shallow--you may have to wade in order not to spook the fish.

Move about 3/4 mile south from Catfish and you'll see the mangroves giving way to the east, which is the start of the Bull Bay archipelago. The grass flats in this area are dotted with infrequent but deep green holes, and if you hit these on falling

NORTH GASPARILLA SOUND

50

water you'll frequently find them populated with nice trout and reds. Captain Pete Greenan and I once encountered a school of 20-pounds-plus reds on this flat, feeding on the bottom half of a spring tide that had their tails out of the water--the date was in late May, not the time when the fish are supposed to be there, which just goes to show you reds don't carry calendars. The big push of reds here normally comes in late summer, when water temperatures exceed 85 degrees.

SANDFLY TO DEVILFISH

After you cross this flat heading south, you drop into the mile-long hole that lies behind Sandfly Key. Water depth is about 4-5 feet compared to 1 foot on the surrounding grass. This stretches all the way to the deeper waters of Charlotte Harbor proper, and because of that it often attracts big-water fish, including tarpon from May through October. The tarpon are not abundant enough to be dependable, but keep your eyes open anytime you pass through and if you see them rolling, stop and show them a MirrOlure.

On low water, this is not a bad spot for a newcomer to drift and cast for trout from November onward through the winter. Use 1/8- to 1/4-ounce plastic swimmer tails, or try some of the classic bucktails like those produced by Bubba--the bulk of these jigs gives them a slow fall that's useful in shallow water.

Devilfish Key has broad shoals on all sides, but there's a 4-foot- deep channel on the eastern tip of the shoal as it nears Cayo Pelau, and a 5-footer running between Devilfish and Sandfly. On the last half of falling water, either of these spots is worth a drift or two. Best way to fish them is to pole the adjacent shallows and cast to the deep water, because if you drift through the deep sections you'll push out any fish that are there.

The entire west shore of Cayo Pelau is worth a look, as well, because the deep water of the hole comes in close to the mangroves. On high spring tides, there are sometimes reds along this shore, and lots more on the south end where the key and the adjoining flat make an elbow known as Little Cape Haze.

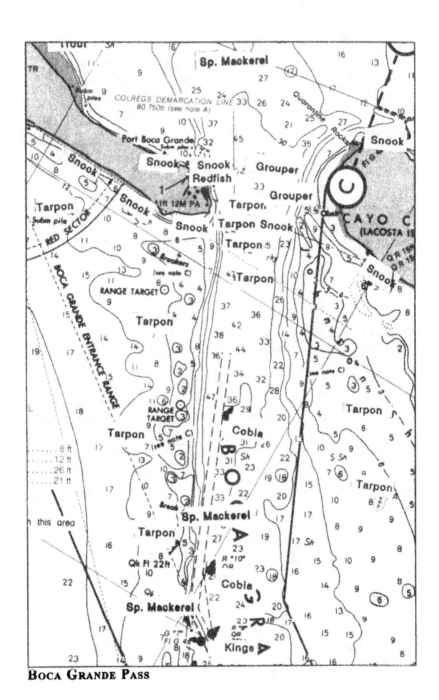

Boca Grande Pass

The south side of Devilfish Key has a grass flat extending up to a half-mile from the island, and from fall through early winter this can be a trout hotspot. One of the guides who knows this area and all of Gasparilla Sound best is Brian Mowatt--see the "Guides" chapter for his phone number.

THE WESTERN SHORE

The western shore of the sound, which is the eastern shore of Gasparilla Island, gets almost no angling attention, which suits all the fish that live there just fine. Beginning at the railroad bridge next to Boca Grande North, there's 4 to 9 feet of water in close to shore for several miles to the south, and any of this can produce on a given day.

The grass on either side of the railroad bridge channel is a good place to look for scaled sardines and the channel itself produces some big trout in spring and fall, sometimes snook in summer. A long bar separates this channel from Peekings Ranch Cove, but if you pass around the tip of this bar you enter a hole that ranges from 6 to 8 feet deep--it's worth checking on winter cold snaps.

Go a bit farther down this shore and you can see the opening of another little bay, this one guarded by a shoal that's only six inches deep on low water, but deep enough to float across on mid- to high tide. Work back in there and skip live sardines around the trees from May through November and you will often be rewarded with snook. The water is as deep as 9 feet in this hole.

AROUND BOCA GRANDE

Proceed a bit further down the shore and you come to the long, dredged boat channel that leads to the town of Boca Grande. The mangroved shores of this 7-foot deep channel look as if they should hold snook, and do produce some on occasion, but it's not the hotspot it appears to be most of the time. However, anywhere there's a downed tree is likely to be a good winter snapper spot--catch them on free-lined live shrimp.

Captain Scott Moore, best known for his snook fishing exploits, shows a 15-pound cobia taken at the Boca Grande Causeway. A variety of species gather at the ends of Gasparilla Sound because of the great inflow of gulf water with each tide.

The flats that make off to the east from this channel occasionally hold redfish, and it's a decent spot for bad weather, because the water is protected all around. The area is not as productive as the richer grass in Bull Bay and other Charlotte Harbor waters, but on high-falling water you'll sometimes find schools of small snook, up to just keeper size, in the cut between Jack Point and Hoagen Key. The approaches are very shallow in this area, so don't stay in there too long unless you're in a high-floater.

Some of the better winter fishing waters in this area are the boat channels that wind through downtown Boca Grande. There's deep water and lots of docks, and the snook love it. You can catch them on topwaters at dawn and dusk, and on live sardines throughout the day. Work along on a trolling motor, casting to all creek and bay mouths, downed trees, rip-rap and overhanging docks. The fish tend to be concentrated in certain areas, absent in others, so move rapidly until you get the first hit, then slow down and work more carefully.

There's a 13-foot-deep hole off the seawall at the golf course, and this can be a winter gathering spot for trout. Bounce a jig along bottom a few times to see if they're in there on chilly December mornings.

Beyond the big-boat channel leading into the Boca Grande yacht basin, a narrow grass flat runs south along the shore toward Boca Grande Pass. This area is consistently productive for trout from March through November. Jigs, topwaters, and small chrome spoons will get them. Fish from about 2 feet on out to where the grass disappears in about 6 feet.

THE PHOSPHATE DOCKS

The famed Phosphate Docks near the southern tip of Gasparilla Island are legendary for monster snook. The docks jut out into 32 feet of water, and the water around them is a morass of hidden pilings, cables and snags. It's snook heaven, home to more 20-pound fish and upward than anywhere else along the west coast.

But getting them out is no game for sissies. Anglers with permission to fish from the docks use 100-pound-test on Calcutta poles. They use a 1-pound sashweight to get their jumbo shrimp or foot-long ladyfish baits down in the 5-knot currents, and when there's a bite, it's an awesome confrontation of muscle. They still lose a lot of fish.

Folks who can't get on the docks--most of us--must anchor on the uptide side on falling water and trail baits back to the pilings. This requires a big anchor and a long anchor rope. Otherwise, your anchor slips and you wind up pinned against the docks--not fun.

Fishing is by far best after dark, by a factor of 100 to 1. You set the anchor, then trail back a pinfish or live sardine on 50-pound grouper tackle, or maybe heavier if you're really serious. Tarpon gear is not out of the question here, the same 80-pound

The grass flats in the Bull Bay area are dotted with infrequent but deep green holes, and if you hit these on falling water you'll frequently find them populated with nice reds.

Dacron they use in the pass. And even then you can't pull some of them clear. It's a different kind of fishing, but there's always action.

The dock also holds schools of jumbo reds in late summer, with the fish averaging 15 pounds and up. They're too big to keep, but fun to exercise. A 1/2- to 1-ounce jig bounced on bottom gets them, as does a heavily-weighted live sardine or pinfish.

GASPARILLA BEACH

Gasparilla Beach is not Gasparilla Sound, but it's near enough for inclusion in this chapter. The beach is a noted spot for snook after the spawn, as the fish move from the passes out into the surf to feed. From late June onward, fishing along the beaches can be dynamite. Anywhere there's rock rip-rap or groins built to slow erosion, snook are likely to stack up. (However, some of the areas that were best in the past were wiped out by the "Hundred Year Storm" in the spring of 1993, and by the following beach replenishment. It may be a season or two before new structure is uncovered.)

On calm summer mornings, you can run your boat right along the inner bar on a trolling motor and cast to the wash of the beach to connect. Even easier is to get out of the boat and walk the beach--but if you do, don't bust your underwear trying to throw to Mexico. The fish are likely to be anywhere from a yard off the beach out to just beyond the first bar, no farther, so throw parallel to the surf as you walk.

WHERE TO STAY AT BOCA GRANDE

Nowhere.

Unless you're son to an oil sheik. The rates for even a modest hotel room are $100 and up. It's financially much wiser to stay on the mainland and run your boat into Gasparilla Sound daily. However, if you can't hack that, there are some reasonable bargains in seasonal packages at Boca Grande North condos. The Waterfront Hotel in downtown Boca Grande is the most convenient spot on the island to stay, with a boat ramp and docks within a few steps of the rooms. The condos at Uncle Henry's Marina at the north end of the island are also convenient for anglers. The best-known marina/tackle shop on the island is Miller's, in downtown Boca Grande, where there's a good selection of all the necessaries, plus a variety of live baits including crabs and squirrelfish if you want to go tarpon fishing. Miller's also has one of the least expensive and best restaurants in town, upstairs overlooking the harbor.

CHAPTER 5

SNOOK OF THE PASSES

"The fish are right there, under the tree. See them?"

I look a little harder, studying the green water like a color-blind pilot trying to pick out the orange numbers, but there is nothing there that I can see, not the subtlest shading, nothing. Scott Moore not only sees them, he can tell how big they are, and, he says, the one off to the right side "has shoulders"--Moor-ish for the mark of a lunker snook.

I flail my bait off in the general direction of the alleged fish, and it drifts a long, boring, unmolested drift down the length of the pass.

He whips out a cast that lands just short of the shadow of the overhanging Australian pine, and his sardine makes it maybe two feet before a snook big enough to swallow a young Labrador inhales it.

"See? They're right there," he observes as the reel squeals and a 20-pounder wallows at the surface.

I have come to pay homage to the guru of snook, an annual pilgrimage sure to make the most elite of fishermen contrite, modest, ashamed of his humble abilities.

Twenty-pound snook like this one caught by Tom Theus of Tampa are common when the fish move into the west coast passes to spawn from May through August. Most are caught on live sardines, though jigs and sinking plugs are also effective, especially after dark.

Moore presents a virtuoso performance at Stump Pass, a take which I have never seen approached. By days end, three anglers have boated more than 60 snook.

Sixty.

Snook.

In one day.

A lot of them are small, smart-alecky 3-pounders that Moore bails aboard and back over the side like undersized crappies.

But quite a few of them are not small, not at all. Several hit the 20-pound mark, one betters 25. There are a whole lot of 6's and 7's.

A year's worth of snook for a common man--and we started late--did I mention we started late? Moore had been having boat trouble, so we didn't get on the water until 9 a.m. And we quit early--at lunch, in fact. Sixty snook in a little over three hours. It sort of leaves you talking to yourself.

THE SUMMER SNOOK FEST

This is not to say that Moore can present this sort of performance every day of the year--and to be sure, I've seen a

The docks and rip rap around Boca Grande Pass are noted for holding monster snook.

few days with him when half-a-dozen fish was it. But from spring through summer, when the fish gather in big schools to spawn, they belong to Scott Moore.

Moore is not the only guide to understand the pattern, to be sure. Larry Mendez, Van Hubbard, Chris Mitchell and others working out of Boca Grande also connect big time--and so do a lot of "amateurs" who fish very well without a guide. Catches of over 100 fish per day have been reported in recent years.

The trick at this time of year is to explore just about any of the larger passes along Florida's southwest coast, looking for the areas where the fish have gathered.

There are fish in every pass, but locating just exactly where in a given pass on a given day separates the men from the boys. Moore has developed the ability to see them, even in water 8 feet deep.

"You look for a patch of water that's darker, for something that's moving, for the flash of a fish's side--there are a lot of clues.''

CHUM THEM UP

Another way to locate them is to chum with live sardines. The baits are injured slightly by squeezing them or bouncing them off the gunnels. The fish blow up on the dizzied, free-drifting baits, and you then slide into casting range and present one with a hook attached.

If you can't see the fish, Moore suggests you keep moving, probing with live bait until you get that first strike. Then, anchor up and work the area hard, because where there's one, there may be 10 . . . or 60, at this time of year.

The prime action continues through the end of August, with new fish coming and going continuously. Fishing the passes is not a secret, by any means, and you'll have lots of company in any flow you choose, but if you have plenty of lively sardines and are persistent in locating the right spot, you'll connect while others go fishless.

RIGGING RIGHT

The best action is usually on the outgoing tide, which brings food past the fish's noses. Cast uptide of the school and let the unweighted bait sweep over them on a 1/0 hook, attached to running line of 8-pound-test or thereabout via 18 inches of 20-pound-test shock leader. Moore suggests the light leader because it gets more strikes than the 30- to 40-pound-test more commonly used.

He also works his baits much like artificials, rather than simply letting them hang in the current.

He often twitches the rod just as the bait lands, sending it skittering and flashing for several feet along the surface. Often, that burst of motion is enough to trigger an instant strike.

He lets the bait sweep over the school, and if it doesn't get a hit, he immediately reels it in and casts uptide again for another drift.

Stump Pass near Englewood is perhaps the most famed snook fishing pass in Florida. Catches of 100 fish per day are sometimes reported by live sardine fishermen.

And one secret of catching high numbers of fish, he says, is to fish a lot of lines.

"When one fish strikes, it excites the others, so you want to have another bait out there for them, rather than having everybody stand there and watch the guy land that first fish," he advises.

The season is closed from June 1 through August 31, so all snook must be released, but for fast snook action, Moore says, there's no hotter time than the dog days of summer.

PRIME PASSES FOR SNOOK

Beginning at Tampa Bay, just about every pass southward will hold spawning snook from mid-May through August. Passage Key Inlet, the southern entrance to Tampa Bay, sometimes offers tremendous action after dark for anglers walking the beach around Bean Point. The water is very deep on the north side of the point, dropping almost straight down into 32 feet of water, but shoals rapidly as you come around to the west side. The point where deep meets shallow is a good spot to hit on incoming tide.

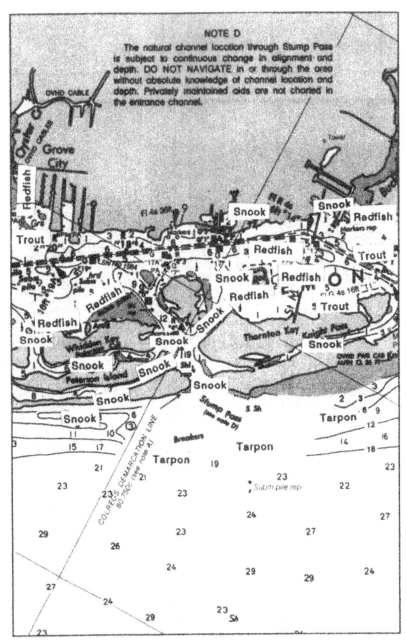

NOTE D

The natural channel location through Stump Pass is subject to continuous change in alignment and depth. DO NOT NAVIGATE in or through the area without absolute knowledge of channel location and depth. Privately maintained aids are not charted in the entrance channel.

STUMP PASS

Use a heavy jig for the deeper water, a topwater to fish the shoal on the west side. There are also abundant snook after dark around the Rod and Reel Pier, just inside Bean Point--they're smart, though, and will only take a live sardine free-lined late at night after most customers have gone home.

As indicated in earlier chapters, Longboat, New and Big Sarasota Pass all offer fine snooking and sometimes some very large fish. Big Sarasota reportedly produced a snook in excess of 50 pounds a few years back. The fish taped better than 60 inches, but was not officially weighed.

Venice Inlet has a number of docks along the south shore from marker 5 landward where you can find action after dark. The rock jetty on the south shore is noted both for big reds and for snook.

Stump Pass is perhaps the most famous of Florida passes for summer snook, though it can be frustrating for first-time visitors. The fish are usually not found in the main pass, although occasionally there are pods around downed trees on the south side. Much more productive are the smaller side passes that make off to the north and south just inside the islands, with the notorious "Ski Alley" on the north the best spot, despite the maddening number of ski boats and personal watercraft that buzz the area constantly. Stump is pretty much a live sardine spot, period, by day, but after dark jigs sometimes work well. There's a slough just off the north beach that can be great after sundown, and after dark the flat inside Whidden Key can be good on a rising tide. Finally, there's a deep channel along the shores of Thornton Key, on the south side of the pass, where fish sometimes hold in close to the mangroves. (If you want to see a ton of big fish, visit the Stump Pass Marina, where you can hand-feed 20-pounders. There's no fishing inside the marina, however.)

Gasparilla Pass, which separates Gasparilla and Little Gasparilla islands, can be a good spot to spoon-jig on an outgoing tide from May through July. The pass splits into three prongs just inside the islands, and the best action is usually found in the north prong, where up to 12 feet of water comes right up

Captiva Pass is a noted snook spot, and you might find fish anywhere along the inside of the pass on the north or south side.

against the docks of the weekend homes on the tip of Little Gasparilla. This is some very serious snooking after dark, with literally hundreds of fish stacked around the better docks. Hit them on the feed and they'll grab most artificials--in the lulls between, live sardines are needed to turn them on. There's also pretty good fishing in the middle prong which passes south of Bird Key before going under the bridge near Boca Grande North condos. You can catch them on a jig from the seawall here at times. (Watch for cobia around this bridge, and around the one on the ICW, in March, April and May.)

For details on Boca Grande Pass, see the chapter on Gasparilla Sound--suffice it to say you won't want to overlook the phosphate docks there in summer. Speaking of the Charlotte Harbor area, though, it should be noted that this is such a large body of water that the fish treat it like the gulf, spawning in small passes leading into the harbor out of the bays. Check the passes into Bull and Turtle bays, as well as the outlet channel at Burnt Store Marina.

Captiva Pass is a noted snook spot, and you might find fish anywhere along the inside of the pass on the north or south side. The bottom is white sand, and by cruising the edges during sunny days, you can often visually pick out schools of fish here--they appear as darker green blobs on the bottom, usually within 30 feet of the drop to deep water. The docks along the south shore are noted for holding some particularly large fish at times.

Redfish Pass was a famed snook spot when summer harvest was allowed, and it's still just as good, but now it's less crowded. The gig here is to fish the outgoing tide, drifting a live shrimp, sardine or pinfish just off bottom. You start the drift just inside Captiva Island, end it just beyond the groins. The idea is to keep the line straight down, so add weight to adjust for current conditions. It's much like fishing for tarpon at Boca Grande, and when the fish are in, you'll catch one per drift.

Blind Pass between Captiva and Sanibel is not much of a pass, but it has 4 to 6 feet of water along the north side, and occasionally produces spring snook. The beaches on both the north and south sides sometimes are worth casting after dark.

San Carlos Bay is really a monster pass, or three passes in one, where the outflows of Pine Island Sound, Matlacha Pass and the Caloosahatchee River meet, and the best fishing is usually in the tributaries rather than in the open pass if you're after snook, though the big water of San Carlos is a fine tarpon spot. Snook sometimes gather near Point Ybel on the south tip of Sanibel, at the north tip of Punta Rassa, and around the bridges.

Big Carlos Pass is broad and deep, and has plenty of fish around the bridge and in both the north and south channel arms. New Pass (there are lots of "New" passes along the southwest coast, thanks to the vagaries of the gulf) is much smaller, but also holds fish in the 7-foot stretches. At Gordon Pass, there's a deep boat basin to the north, and the outlet of this area is often very good. Also check the 5-foot-deep cut that hooks south around Marker 6, just inside the pass.

There's also fine pass fishing in the many passes around the Marco area. For details, see Chapter 15.

CHAPTER 6

CATCH AND RELEASE
GROUPER AT SARASOTA

Nobody in their right mind would let the sea's most sought finny fillets swim off, if they were legal sized and not in excess of the bag limit.

Would they?

Richard Nutter and Terry Copeland of Sarasota do it almost every weekend, and the fish they release would make many an old-time grouper-digger sob. They regularly put back gags of 20 pounds, reds of 15.

Nutter, a lanky taxidermist with a ready grin, says he's not squirrely, not by a long shot. But he gets too big a kick out of dukeing it out with a hulking 30-incher to fish out his secret honey holes, just for bragging rights back at the docks.

"When I found out it may take 20 years or more to replace a fish in the 15- to 20-pound class, it made me stop and think. When you pull all the big ones off a rock, there aren't going to be any more growing up to provide that thrill again for a decade or more. When you think about all the money you have in a boat, tackle, and the gas to run it, it starts to look like the crazy anglers are the ones that fish out their numbers."

So, for the last three years, Nutter and Copeland, a furniture company executive, have been putting back most of the big fish they catch.

"When you have one of these spots that consistently turns out big fish, it changes your whole attitude. You want to protect those fish and take care of them, because they'll be there every time you go back to provide you with sport," Copeland says.

Not that the two anglers are teetotalers when it comes to release fishing. They like grouper filets too much for that, and they also like to compete in local grouper tournaments.

"We'll take the 20- to 24-inch fish to eat, three or four for each of us, and that's all we need to bring back to the docks," says Copeland. "Now and then we get a big one that is injured, and we bring those in, too, so our freezers are never without filets, but we're not taking nearly what we could. If more people operated the same way, I think we'd see a boom in big grouper out there, just like we've seen a redfish boom inshore since catches have been limited."

Copeland said that saving the fish also puts them in a great position on tournament day, because they know exactly where to go to connect with the lunkers that are likely to win. Tournaments in the area limit the take to three fish per boat, so there's no problem with decimating the hotspots by taking tourney fish.

The anglers fish from Nutter's 30-foot Wellcraft Scarab, a narrow stiletto of a boat powered by twin Evinrude 235's. The speed of this rig makes it possible for them to get offshore quickly and check a lot of spots on their way, and Nutter says that's part of the secret of finding big fish.

"For catch and release to work, you have to find numbers that aren't in the published lists and that aren't known to other captains in the area. That means you have to constantly be on the lookout for new spots, little spots that are hard to find. If you locate a dozen or so of those areas over a year of fishing, it's like money in the bank, but you have to stop hundreds of times over

Locating your own grouper spots is a matter of keeping an eye on the depthfinder continuously, and of making dozens of stops. It's also important not to clean out your rockpiles, once you find them.

likely-looking bottom to find that many good spots. It's like any thing else, you have to pay your dues.''

Nutter says he believes big fish attract big fish, and often a reef that holds one 20-pounder will hold lots of them, and few smaller ones.

''A three-pounder has got to be uncomfortable around fish with mouths big enough to swallow him whole, so he sort of avoids the big-fish reefs. I know if I catch several little ones from a spot, it's probably not going to hold a lot of big ones.''

Copeland admits that the team occasionally loses a hole to other anglers who blunder into it, and thus the fish they release wind up in somebody else's ice chest.

"It's a chance you take," he notes. "But by releasing these fish, we're having great sport and still can go home and feel good about the day, not having hurt the resource. It's worth the risk that now and then some fish hog is going to luck up on your spot and wipe out the population."

In a typical day, the anglers load up the flow-through baitwell at the transom around dawn with pinfish, grunts and squirrelfish from inshore rock piles. By 8 a.m., they're 20 miles offshore in 70 feet of water, aimed at one of their secret numbers. But they'll probably make a dozen stops before they get there, because every time they note a spike of fish on the Si-Tex recorder, they stop, motor over it a few times, and if the spike looks like fish instead of just bait, they drop down a pair of live baits.

Their tackle is light stuff for most grouper fishermen, short "stand-up" rods about five feet long, the reels Shimano Triton 20's and 30's, filled with 30-pound mono. An egg sinker of about 8 ounces goes on the end of the running line, held there by a stout barrel swivel. A length of 100-pound-test mono just long enough to allow the 9/0 hook to be attached to the reel seat when not in use completes the rig. They also make use of 6- to 8-ounce white bucktail jigs at times, often tipping them with a live squirrelfish-- an offering that Richard says is a favorite for really big grouper.

Nutter says that the "Christmas tree" marking that some anglers talk about is not what he looks for on the chart paper when he's seeking big fish.

"That Christmas tree is usually bait, not grouper," he observes. "The grouper show up as a thin vertical line extending maybe 10 to 20 feet off the bottom, or sometimes as a number of individual marks around a ledge that may measure anywhere from three to eight feet high."

Nutter doesn't drop anchor very often, unless wind and current are moving the boat too rapidly for efficient fishing. Usually, he drifts over the mark with the baits slipping along just

Fast, twin-engined boats make it possible to cover a lot of water in a day, and the skipper who keeps a careful log of spots, both in his loran or GPS and on paper, will soon build up many prime locations that are virtually unfished.

a few feet off bottom. He constantly kicks the reel out of gear, letting the sinker plummet back to bottom instead of kiting out behind with the drift of the boat.

"If I make two drifts right over top of a spike of fish and don't get bit, I'll go look for something else," he says. "When you're on them, big grouper let you know they're down there right away."

He says another reason he's slow to anchor is that if another boat approaches while he's into fish, it's easy to drift away from the spot and keep them from LORANing him. When other boats are in sight, he uses a gray marker buoy about the size of a baseball to pinpoint the location where the fish are holding.

Make your search for grouper well offshore. The farther out you get, the less competition you'll have from other boats who prune off all the inshore keepers before they reach lunker size.

"People think if they get your numbers within a couple of hundred feet, they can come back to that spot and catch fish. Usually, they can't. Your sonar cone is just a few feet wide in 80 feet, and it's really hard to get right on a spot, sometimes even if you've got the exact numbers. In fact, I think that's what separates the men from the boys sometimes, is just having the patience once you get on a likely spot to work back and forth over it until you hit that one little area where they're all stacked up."

When a grouper is caught, they work it to the surface fairly slowly, to avoid excessive gas build-up in the bladder. Even at that, nearly all of the fish must have their stomach punctured through the mouth and the bladder punctured by going through the belly near the vent. The anglers say that numerous studies have shown that such deflation does no long-term damage to most fish, and it's essential if they're to swim back to the bottom before sharks find them.

They tag most fish that they release, and Nutter said that the tags prove that many punctured fish survive. They've caught and released many of their "pet" fish several times.

(Incidentally, neither angler accepts the idea that when you let a grouper get away or break off, it warns others on the reef not to eat by grunting. They report that releasing fish seems to have no effect on those still below, which remain eager to bite most of the time.)

The reds are much more durable than the gags, Copeland notes. For some reason, the reds almost always dash back toward bottom the minute they're put back into the water, but the gags often require a certain amount of pumping to circulate water over their gills before they come back to life, and sometimes they don't make it, despite the best efforts of the angler. If the boat has drifted far off the rock, they usually try to motor back to the spot quickly before releasing the fish, since a tired grouper without a hole nearby is an easy target for sharks.

For those interested in starting their own catch-and-release grouper spots, Nutter and Copeland offer the following suggestions.

1. Don't be satisfied with catching little fish. The reefs with big ones are still out there, but it takes persistence to find them. If you spend your time catching little ones, you'll never discover the spots where the big ones live.

2. Make your search well offshore. The farther out you get, the less competition you'll have from other boats who prune off all the inshore keepers before they reach lunker size.

3. Avoid fishing weekends if you can. If you do find a honey hole and there are a lot of other boats nearby, somebody is sure to take note of your luck and get your numbers.

4. When there are other boats nearby, use an unobtrusive marker buoy to pinpoint the spot. Big, bright buoys are easily seen at a distance by other boatmen.

5. Handle your catches quickly and gently. Use thin wire to make the puncture in stomach and bladder, then get them back over the side promptly.

"We aren't ever going to see the good old days of grouper fishing again, where everybody could go out there and load up 300 or 400 pounds a day and come back to sell them," says Terry Copeland. "But if we conserve what we've got, we can still have quality bottom fishing, despite the pressure of modern angling."

CHAPTER 7

BULL BAY

Two of the most interesting areas around Charlotte Harbor are the broad, shallow bays on the northwest side, Bull and Turtle.

Bull Bay is the shallower of the two, with almost no water more than 3 feet deep with the exception of the entry channels, which have as much as 9 feet.

Bull is created by a barrier of mangrove islands, including Cayo Pelau, the largest, cutting it off from the deep, open water of Charlotte Harbor proper. These islands and the extremely shallow water have kept Bull from getting over-run by casual fishermen, though these days there are lots of flats boats working the area, particularly on weekends.

The clarity of the water and the fishing pressure makes it no place for amateurs. Despite high fish numbers, it's very possible to spend a full day in Bull and never get a hit, and lots of weekenders do just that.

On the other hand, pros who regularly fish these waters, including captains Scott Moore, Chris Mitchell, Brian Mowatt, Bill Miller and Larry Mendez, have tremendous success there.

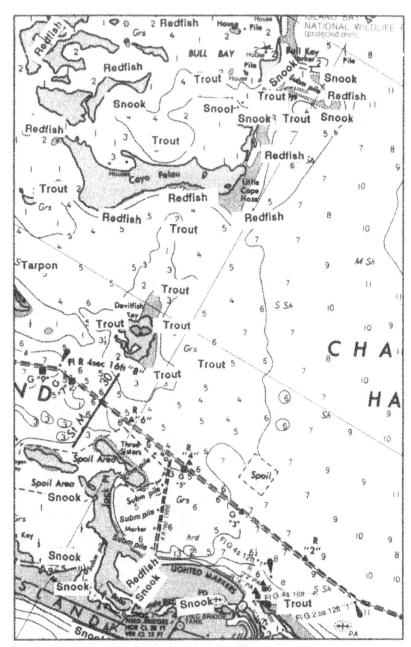

BULL BAY AND LOWER GASPARILLA SOUND

On strong tide flows, several oyster bars dotting the deeper water are frequently good areas to pick up big snook or redfish.

Captains Pete Greenan and Van Hubbard do, too, which proves your last name does not have to start with an ''M'' to catch fish in Bull Bay, I guess.

The normal procedure is to fish the two entry channels on falling water, when fish from the flats often pull into these deeper areas to feed and rest, and then move to the shallows on the rise.

The channels are unmarked, but can readily be located, running east through Charlotte Harbor along the white bar south of Cayo Pelau, because a long sandbar extends nearly a half-mile into the harbor between the two cuts. Getting into the west cut takes a bit of a jump over the bar, which may only be a foot under water at low tide, but once you're inside, there's at least 4 feet all the way back to the deeper basin where the two channels join. The edges of this channel are a good area to work a topwater on rising water for trout, while the channel itself is good on the fall with jigs or slow-sinking plugs like the 52M or the Rattlin' Flash. (It's often eaten up with ladyfish and jacks, so if you don't like to catch these guys between trout, you may have to seek other waters.)

The east channel is easier to get into, with depths of about 2 feet on the bar, dropping quickly to 7 to 9 feet on the inside. Some of the deepest water is at the narrowest point between Bull Key and the mangroved oyster bar that splits the two entry channels, and this area can be a hotspot for snook if you're tossing live sardines or free-lining shrimp. The fish here are usually too sophisticated for an artificial, however. On falling water at dawn, dusk or after dark, you might also do well to work the north edge of the drop here, which is where a lot of the water falls off the flats to exit the bay.

The Bull Bay hole extends north and west from the passes, with average depth of around 4 feet. You'll note the old fishing shack sitting on pilings at the west edge of the hole--imagine the fishing that must have gone on here 30 years ago! Incidentally, that shack looks like it should have snook stacked around the worm-eaten pilings that hold it up, but I've never managed to catch one out from under it. There are often fish along the shoreline behind it, though.

There are several oyster bars dotting the deeper water, and on strong tide flows these are frequently good areas to pick up big snook and redfish. You'll often find trout in the hole, as well, particularly from November through February--provided you happen to visit on a day when the netters haven't cleaned it out.

Fishing shacks in Bull Bay are within casting distance of prime snook spots. The deeper basins produce on low tide, while the flats are excellent on high.

There's a fairly deep, grassy slough that's neither hole nor flat on the west side of the main pool of Bull, and this often holds trout, including the occasional 5-pounder, in spring.

Looking north from the slough, you see what looks like a mini-Everglades, an unmarked morass of very shallow water and winding creeks between mangrove islands. It's untouched by human habitation, a part of Island Bay National Wildlife Refuge alive with birds, exotic plants--and fish. It's no place for a deep-draft boat, but if your hull will float in a foot or less and run in about 18 inches, you're ok in there on mid- to high tide.

Because you might spot fish almost anywhere in these shallows, the best program for learners is to go in on pushpole or trolling motor, watching from the platform for tailing reds or for snook loafing in the yellow sand holes. You need a long-cast spinning outfit to reach the fish at a distance, before they sense the boat. A 1/2 ounce gold spoon makes the long casts easier and won't be passed up by the redfish. Heavy, bullet-shaped topwaters are also good, with the Rat-Lure, Mini-Spook and Bagley Finger Mullet all effective.

If you're good with a flyrod and like wadefishing, stake out your boat and wade your heart out--you can go for miles in here, never hitting a channel that's deeper than your waist. You'll find reds and trout in a fair number of the holes from October through April--but most of them, obviously, will be empty. The trick is to keep going until you hit a "live" hole--it's likely to hold reds, trout, and ladyfish in winter and maybe some snook in fall, spring and summer. For reasons known only to themselves, the fish ignore similar holes all around these hotspots, and will be in that particular spot day after day until a weather change or fishing pressure moves them. So, if you locate two or three of these spots, you've got a lock on it. Shrimp imitations are the best offerings in winter, sardine-like lures spring through fall.

In general, the hot holes are likely to be on the island points or in the cuts with strongest tide flows, but in this country you never know--the guy with the best eyes and the most patience wins.

It's very possible to get temporarily lost when you get back into Bull a mile or so, but if you remember that the water flow has scoured the channels generally north and south, you'll eventually work your way out. Just be sure to start looking before the tide begins to fall, because many of the basins between islands become completely landlocked on low spring tides, or when strong northeast winds push the tides beyond the usual lows. Several of my friends have enjoyed an unplanned night in there while the mosquitoes enjoyed them--trust me, it's better to stay at the Waterfront.

There are a couple of slightly deeper basins as you approach the north end of Bull Bay, cuddled up against the south side of the largest mangrove island. This area frequently holds snook and reds in spring and fall. If you get back into this zone and don't want to pick your way out, you can get out the "back way" by going west into the Whidden Creek basin, where you can jump on plane in 3 feet of water and then run west into Gasparilla

In general, the hot holes are likely to be on the island points or in the cuts with strongest tide flows, but you never know--the guy with the best eyes and the most patience wins.

Sound. (Careful, though--here, as elsewhere, there are plenty of flats you can't get across on low water.)

There are also some deeper basins on the east side of Bull Bay, just before it joins the open water of Turtle Bay. These can be good areas on low tides, and the oyster bars around the points are good on rising water for reds and trout.

In general, you can usually pick up scattered reds and the occasional snook, spring through fall, by casting to the mangroves on high tides. It's a good strategy for first-timers just learning the water, because if you stay at it for a couple of hours, you'll inevitably hit a pod or two of fish.

A popping cork rig with a jig, like Love's Float-N-Jig or the Mansfield Mauler, does a good job of pulling fish out of the trees--toss it up close, bloop it to get their attention and make the jig hop, and watch the cork for signs of a take. You can do the same thing with live shrimp, which will also catch you some mangrove snapper in fall.

In general, throughout Bull Bay, the fish gather where there's something a bit different from the surrounding flats--an island point or channel that concentrates tide flow, deeper water along a mangrove edge, a shell bar that creates a hunting ground for crabs--keep your eyes open, and you'll find plenty of likely targets. Many days, there will be no need ever to leave Bull to have a super fishing trip.

CHAPTER 8

TURTLE BAY

Turtle Bay is a deeper and wider basin than Bull Bay, and looks more like a true bay rather than like a northerly annex of the Everglades. Its eastern shore is formed by the low peninsula that makes up Cape Haze, while the west side is a scatter of islands that lets into Bull Bay. Like Bull, Turtle is guarded on the south by shallow water with only a few breaks deep enough to allow a boat on plane to enter.

Once you get inside, however, there's lots of open water where navigation is easy, and where those who don't like leaning on a pushpole all day will find relatively easy fishing.

THE ENTRIES

One of the entries is near the eastern end of the string of islands that mark the bay's southern boundary and cut it off from Charlotte Harbor proper. Here, there's a long, curved bar extending into the harbor, and two small islands, with a longer mangrove island extending off to the west. The entrance is

BULL BAY AND TURTLE BAY

The cut off Charlotte Harbor can be a tremendous spot for snook because it attracts spawning fish--not uncommon for deeper sloughs in bays far from the Gulf passes.

obvious, a deep green cut when the sun is up, with as much as 10 feet of water down the middle.

This cut can be a tremendous spot for snook in May, June and July, because it attracts spawning fish--not uncommon for deeper sloughs in bays far from the Gulf passes. It's primarily a live

brown water. Each of these bars holds fish at times, though they're all obvious spots and get plenty of pressure.

In spring they're good for large trout, while from August through November they usually attract redfish. There are always flounder around, as well. The determinant of whether the bars are "on" is baitfish--if there's lots of bait flipping around them, there will be fish there somewhere. The bars particularly hold young mullet throughout all but the coldest months, and since these forage fish attract larger gamefish, the bars are sometimes good spots to pick up a trophy. If you don't see lots of bait on them--and the baitfish come and go without evident reason, just like other species--it might be better to check other spots.

A small spoon like the Cotee or the Champ is one of the best offerings here--toss it long and start cranking BEFORE it hits the surface, so that it doesn't sink and snag the shells. Work the lure from the shallowest edges on out to 3 feet of water. Topwaters also work well.

Most anglers drift the bars and cast to them, and that works, but because of the shallow water, you only get a couple of good drifts before the boat spooks the fish this way. Better is to drop the anchor as soon as you catch the first fish, work that area over thoroughly, and then let the boat drift only about 50 feet before anchoring down again. (You can't "stake out" in most of the areas here because the bottom is too hard for a push pole.)

Or, if you have thick-soled, high-topped wading shoes, get out and crunch along the bar--the very best way to fish this area. (Obviously, you don't try this in your flip-flops unless you enjoy chumming for sharks with your own blood.) Walking the bars allows casting to both sides with ease, and there are days when you can spend an entire high tide in there and have good fishing pretty much throughout as you keep circling the shell mounds.

Turtle extends several miles to the north, and there's plenty of depth up there as backcountry goes, average about 3 feet and some areas as deep as 6. This can be a good area to drift for trout in spring and fall, but it gets too brackish and tannin-stained after the summer rains begin in June and on through August. You

If you have thick-soled, high-topped wading shoes, get out and crunch along the bar--the very best way to fish this area. Walking the bars allows casting to both sides with ease, and there are days when you can spend an entire high tide in there and have good fishing pretty much throughout as you keep circling the shell mounds.

might see young tarpon here at this time, however--fish them where you see them roll. There are shallow creeks on the northeast end, and you'll find an occasional redfish and trout in there in winter--and complete solitude.

The "elbow" where Turtle cuts off to the north often has some cruising snook and reds around the point, and around the old fishing shack just on the south side of this point. This water gets very clear in winter, and the fish are wise to the ways of anglers, so it's essential to beach the boat on the north side of the point and slip back along the shore to make a successful presentation. You'll need live sardines to turn them on, too, unless you go after dark.

The west/central part of Turtle looks more like Bull Bay, with a scatter of small islands, cuts and basins, all of them worth prospecting for trout and reds pretty much year around. With a shallow-draft boat and a high tide, you can enter the backcountry on the west shore of Turtle and run all the way into Gasparilla Sound without ever moving out of protected water, a handy trick because the most easily-accessible boat ramps in this area are at the Boca Grande bridge, on the northwest end of Gasparilla Sound, and on those days when 20-knot winds are howling, nobody wants to make the ride down the sound and out into the open harbor to get at Bull or Turtle bay fishing.

CHAPTER 9

FISHING THE GRANDE PASS

For sheer numbers of tarpon, there's probably no match anywhere on the planet for Boca Grande.

The deep, broad pass about 90 miles south of Tampa gets absolutely stiff with hundred-pound tarpon from May through July each year, so many fish that first-timers often think their chart recorders are on the fritz as the screen turns black from bottom to top marking fish. In a four-hour tide, it's not uncommon to see 1,000 or more fish rolling at the surface, and those that show represent only a small portion of those that are stacked into the 72-foot depths of the pass.

This is not exactly a secret, as you might suspect.

The tiny village of Boca Grande, on the north side of the pass, comes alive during the flurry. Roads that are usually empty become jammed, marinas and bait shops fill up, and there are waiting lines at every restaurant. Fishing goes on 24 hours a day, with the action often best after sundown, when the lights from dozens of boats bobbing in the pass create a glow that looks like a miniature city, gliding slowly through the night.

Fishing in the clustered fleet, you may see anybody from United States Senators to rock stars to NFL quarterbacks, all staring intently at their rod tips, listening closely to the captain's commands of "green on the tip" or "red on the reel".

Here, no matter who you are, you listen to the skipper if you want to catch fish.

TECHNIQUES FOR "THE GRAND PASS"

Most tarpon are caught on live bait at the pass. According to Captain Jon Zorian of the charterboat Viper 4, the favorites are mutton minnows and squirrel fish during the day, "pass crabs" or "dollar crabs" at night. The latter are small crabs about the size of a silver dollar, which flow out of the back country of Charlotte Harbor in incredible numbers during the spring tarpon run. They're readily netted in the pass.

Live jumbo shrimp are also a good bait. Some of the guides depend on them in May, particularly during slack tide periods when the fish refuse all other baits.

Curiously, most guides don't bother to fish for tarpon where they see them rolling. The theory is that the rollers are "playing" and are not interested in food. Those massed closer to bottom, on the other hand, are likely to take, so the skippers pay a lot more attention to the tarpon they see on their depthfinders than those they see on top.

In general, the feeding fish are most often found on the ledge of the up-current side of the deeper holes, so the top skippers spend a lot of time working over these locations, pinpointing them by lining up the Boca Grande Lighthouse and the fuel storage tanks ashore as rangemarkers for the various hotspots. The baits are fished on heavy gear, weighted with adequate lead to keep them just off bottom.

TACKLE FOR THE PASS

Most guides fish 80-pound-test Dacron on 50-pound-class tackle, primarily Penn International reels and stout, 6 to 7 foot roller-guide rods. The heavy Dacron doesn't stretch on hook

The famed lighthouse at Boca Grande Pass marks what is probably the world's best tarpon hole. The 72-foot deep pass holds thousands of fish from May through July.

sets, and has the power to control the fish amidst the heavy boat traffic. The "undersized" reels are used because they are lighter and easier to handle than 80's, and because vast line capacity is not necessary for tarpon in the pass, which rarely get more than 200 yards from the boat.

Captain Jon Zorian's favorite rigging approximates that used by most skippers in the pass: The line is tied into a number 5 brass swivel, and the leader, 12 feet of Number 7 wire, is connected to the swivel with a haywire twist. The wire is preferred to mono, even though tarpon have no teeth, because its density keeps it closer to the bottom of the pass. Mono leaders tend to "balloon" upward in the four- to six-knot current common on peak tide flows.

The weight, anywhere from 2 to 8 ounces depending on current, is attached to the swivel with a few wraps of light copper wire. When a tarpon jumps, the weight is usually thrown clear, so that it doesn't act as a bolo to jerk the hook from the fish's mouth.

Most guides use 5/0 forged Mustad hooks, style 7690, file-sharpened for instant penetration. Gamakatsu live bait hooks are also becoming popular--their semi-circular form seems to consistently hook and hold, particularly when fishing live crabs.

Boca Grande guides stitch bits of colored yarn into their line to act as markers for the length of line to be let out to keep the bait very close to bottom, but not close enough to snag the jumbles of rocks. A bit of green yarn is inserted at 42 feet, a bit of red at 60 feet. Added to the 12-foot leader length, this makes just the right total for fishing either the shallower ledges or the 72-foot maximum depth. The skipper controls the depths of the bait by instructing the client to put "green on the tip", "green on the reel" or "red on the tip", "red on the reel." It's a handy shorthand that avoids most snags, yet keeps the bait in the strike zone most of the time.

THE HOOK-UP

When a tarpon takes, there's no mistaking it. The heavy rod takes on an alarming bend, and as soon as it does the skipper firewalls the throttle. This takes up slack, drives the hook home, and gets the boat out of the way in case the fish decides to come straight up and jump, as they often do.

"The one problem a lot of beginners have is that they want to jerk on the rod to set the hook," notes Jon Zorian. "You can't jerk hard enough to get all the slack out and drive the barb home, but you can jerk hard enough to make him spit out the bait. My customers keep their hands on top of the rod, not under it, so they can't reflexively set the hook when they get a strike."

Zorian also adds a length of split plastic hose to the lower section of his rods, where they cross the gunnel, to give a bit of cushioning and to prevent the rod from slipping at the strike.

Once a fish is hooked, the boat is quickly jockeyed to the side of the pass, so the fight can go on without tangling in the dozens of lines from other boats. Fights tend to be brutal and short, with 20 minutes about average for a 90-pound fish. When the fish is brought to boatside, the skipper uses gloved hands to control the leader and either removes the hook or snips the wire as far down as he can reach.

Biologists studying radio-tagged fish have learned that most survive this procedure without permanent harm, and in fact, most go right back to the pass within an hour or two.

JIGGING THE PASS

These days, a few anglers specialize in jigging the pass, and even the old hard-line Boca Granders are starting to switch over, because the jigs work better than live baits on occasion.

Most use jigs weighing from 1 to 4 ounces, built on long-shank 5/0 to 7/0 hooks. Large plastic "swimmer tails" from Cotee, Bubba or 12-Fathom are added to provide color and action. Two feet of 80-pound-test mono is used as shock leader against the rough jaws of the fish.

Using either medium saltwater spinning gear with 25-pound-test or revolving spool reels with 30 to 40-pound test, the jigs are tossed down-current as far as possible in an area where the depthfinder shows lots of fish. The jig is allowed to sink as the angler takes in slack, with the boat drifting toward the spot where the jig hit the water. As soon as the jig touches bottom, it's jigged upward in a series of short twitches. You get perhaps 15 to 20 seconds of "bottom time" for each cast, not much, but often it's enough. As soon as the jig stops making bottom contact, it's reeled up and cast ahead of the drift once again.

No one is sure why, but some days, the jig fishermen are busy continuously, while live baiters go to sleep on their rods. It's not often that way, but it happens frequently enough that most serious pass anglers now carry jigging gear just in case.

FLY-LINING

"Fly-lining" is not fly fishing, not as it's practiced at Boca Grande. There are times when the fish feed on the surface, gulping down the thousands of crabs that drift through the pass. It's obvious when this is happening, because rather than seeing

Whether you fish live bait or jigs, day or night, Boca Grande is a trip--one every angler ought to experience at least once in his life.

the fish roll like porpoises, you see hearty explosions as they blast the bait.

When this is going on, the best place for your bait is on top, and the best bait for your hook is one of the crabs, readily dipped up with a long-handled net. The crabs are drifted with the tide on mono leaders, unweighted, the boat bumped in and out of gear to prevent drag from ruining the natural drift of the bait. Sometimes a quarter-ounce of lead is added to keep the bait slightly beneath the surface, but in general the presentation is made either on top or in the upper three feet of the water column.

All fish caught by any method are released to fight again-- though you can order a fiberglass replica of your fish at the docks, if you like. Some 5,000 tarpon per year are caught here, and virtually none are killed thanks to conservation-conscious anglers.

Whether you fish live bait or jigs, day or night, Boca Grande is a trip--one every angler ought to experience at least once in his life. You'll never see more tarpon anywhere, and you'll never have a better chance of catching one.

PASS ETIQUETTE

There are days when more than a hundred boats jam into the pass, drifting close enough to bump rubrails.

Basically, you have to drift with the wind and tide over the length of the hole, maintaining your distance and traveling along with all the other boats in the fleet--you manage this by keeping the engine running and bumping it in and out of gear to maintain steerage and keep your lines going straight down instead of ballooning out behind the boat. One angler must devote all his time to handling the boat, watching the depthfinder, and keeping an eye on the traffic.

When a drift is completed, you pick up your lines and motor in a wide, low-speed arc outside the drifting fleet, rather than running right back up through them. A single boat going the wrong direction at speed has the same effect as a wrong-way drunk on an interstate highway.

The Boca Grande Fishing Guides Association has produced a brochure detailing these procedures and also telling exactly how to rig to fish the pass. You can get this free brochure by sending a stamped, self-addressed envelope to Boca Grande Fishing Guides Association, P.O. Box 676, Boca Grande, FL 33921. The leaflet also contains the names and phone numbers of all charterboat captains, in case you want to learn first-hand how it's done.

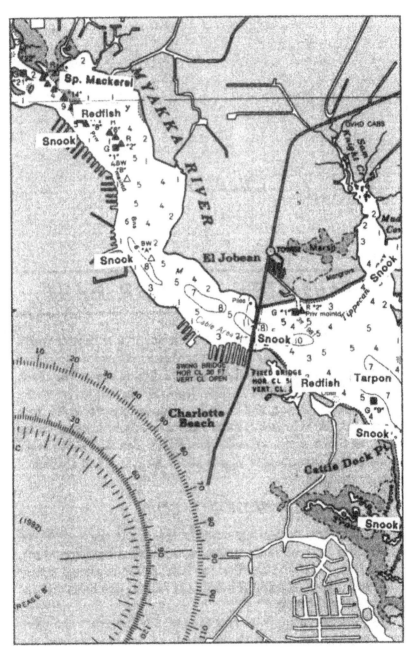

MYAKKA RIVER

possibility. For the last few years, action has been slower, but still good enough to make it worth a trip.

The fish might be anywhere from Cape Haze northward, but the 20-foot deep hole that begins roughly due west of the channel into Burnt Store Marina is a good place to start. Fish often gather in the 23-foot hole that is south/southwest of marker 1, in the center of the Harbor just off Punta Gorda. They roam up the Myakka at least to the bridge at El Jobean, and into the Peace River to the U.S. 41 bridge in good numbers, with strays working their way up to the I-75 bridge in late summer.

Cruise slowly and keep moving until you see rolling fish, bubbles, the tip of a fin--any clue that big fish are plowing along close to the surface. If you don't see any rollers, seek out bait concentrations--and the bait need not be tarpon-sized. Sometimes the fish go bonkers over glass minnows, scooping the inch-long fish into their mouths like cruising whales. During the hottest feeds, you'll sometimes see tarpon free-jumping, blasting through the bait and making enormous, grey-hounding leaps as they feed.

There are two ways to connect with them. Most interesting is to use a small boat and a powerful trolling motor to slide within casting range of rolling fish. Using a 52- or 65-M MirrOlure, the trick is to place the lure far enough in front of rolling fish so that it sinks down to their level by the time they cruise past it. Captain Bill Miller is a master at the art, jumping dozens of fish each season on the minnow-like plugs.

"If the fish are making shallow rolls, they're traveling pretty fast," says Miller. "If they're making steeper rolls or just bumping their heads up above the surface, they're moving slower or maybe not moving forward at all. You learn to gauge their speed and adjust your cast accordingly. When they're going fast, you might have to cast 50 feet ahead of them to allow time for the plug to sink by the time they approach."

The fish are large, averaging 90 to 110 pounds. Other guides who specialize in this fishing, like Captain Paul Hawkins from St. Petersburg, prefer a very stiff, 7-foot baitcaster loaded with 20-pound-test line. A shock leader of 100-pound-test is used to

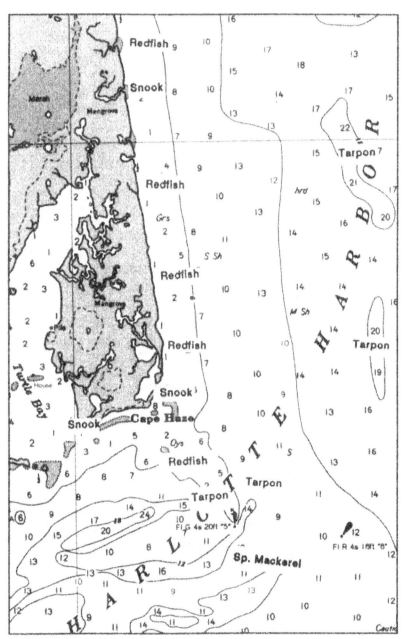

CAPE HAZE

104

prevent the fish's jaws from abrading the line, and a leader of 30-pound-test mono about 10 feet long is usually tied in ahead of the running line to protect the line from tail-whipping. Best reels are the Ambassadeur 7000 and similars, which have plenty of line to control most fish despite the hair-raising first runs.

When the fish are more scarce or less active, cut bait often stirs them into feeding. Fresh menhaden or "shad" is the favored bait. Several handfuls are chopped up and scattered behind the anchored boat in an area where fish have been seen rolling, and a whole shad is fished on bottom on 30- to 40-pound gear. The 7/0 Gorilla Big Game Hook, a circle hook from Worth, is one of the most effective hooks you can use for getting a good hookup in this sort of fishing. Most anglers like to put out a "spider web" of up to eight rods all around the boat. You catch a lot of sailcats this way, but you also catch a lot of tarpon.

The tarpon usually disappear by late October, but plenty of redfish are prowling the creeks and bars on the east side of the harbor by then, and the fall run of trout into the back side is just weeks away, so there's plenty to entertain fishermen.

SNOOK ON THE BACK SIDE

Snook are also abundant on the "dogleg" of Charlotte Harbor, with tremendous catches sometimes made around the mouths of the larger creeks and sloughs from May through July as the fish gather to spawn. These backwater fish, rather than migrating to the Gulf passes to drop their eggs, simply find deep, high-flow areas near their usual residences and spawn there.

One of the prime secret spots is the entrance canal to Burnt Store Marina. The waters between and around the rockpiles here hold loads of fish in summer, particularly on the new and full moons--topwaters get them early and late, live sardines at other times. (Burnt Store is a good place to stay, too, with a full-service marina, ramp, docks and condominium or motel accommodations.) The outflow from Alligator Creek, just south of Punta Gorda on the east shore, is also worth checking, though not so much a sure thing as Burnt Store.

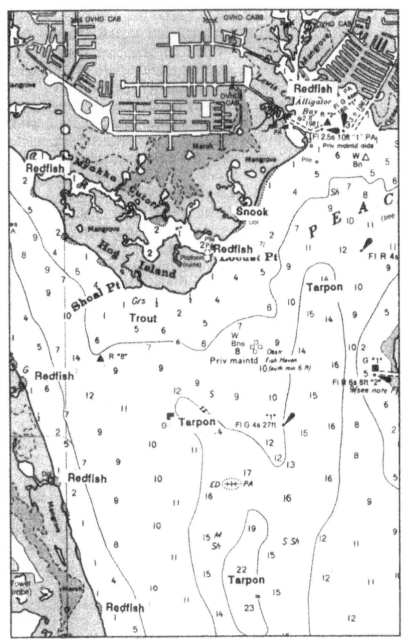

NORTH CHARLOTTE HARBOR

Captain Paul Hawkins puts a silver king into the air off Port Charlotte. Many fish migrate to the back section of Charlotte Harbor in late summer, and remain there into October.

In winter, hundreds of these snook move into the Peace and the Myakka rivers, where they provide outstanding plug casting. The fish go up at least to the I-75 bridge on the Myakka. On the Peace, they've been caught as far up as Wauchula, more than 40 miles inland! Work the side creeks on the Peace, including the Lettuce Lake Cutoff, Hunter Creek and Shell Creek, plus the mouths of smaller creeks on the falling tides. You can also find fish by trolling diving plugs, and by drifting with live shiners. Most fish will run small, 20- to 24-inchers, but some fish over 25 and even 30 pounds are taken in the rivers each winter. The fishing usually begins in mid-November, peaks between Thanksgiving and Christmas.

THE WESTERN SHORE

The west shore of the harbor is unique for a Florida shoreline, running in an almost unbroken straight line for nearly 10 miles.

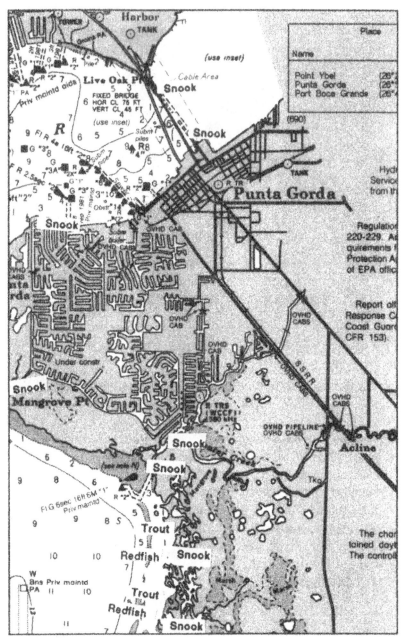

PUNTA GORDA

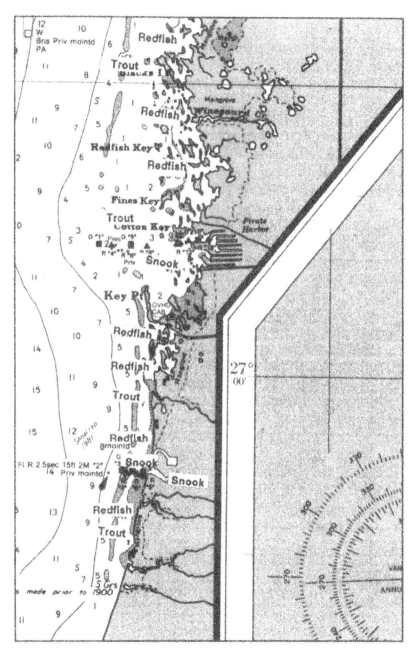

CHARLOTTE HARBOR, EASTERN SHORE

At first glance, this makes it seem an unlikely area to fish, but there's a grassy shoal that extends at least a quarter mile from shore before falling off to the black depths of the main harbor, and this area frequently holds redfish in late summer.

An easy way to find them is to run the edge of the flats on a calm morning, watching for the fish to "chill up" or start to move as they hear the approaching motor. A school makes a ripple that is readily visible for several hundred yards, and if you stay on the outer edge of the flats, your high-speed run won't harm the grass or push the fish out.

Reds--and snook as well--are most often found on the shell flats around the mouths of the many small creeks that open into the harbor here. Best action is usually on outgoing tides in these areas. Some of the creeks are navigable for only a couple hundred yards, but a few, like Trout Creek near Cattle Dock Point on the north end, extend for over a mile back into the mangroves. The larger creeks hold snook frequently, though you have to pole the boat and make long casts to avoid spooking them. Most of these creeks have shallow bars at their mouths, though there's deeper water inside. Make sure you don't go up the creek on high tide and get yourself stuck there as the water falls--on spring lows, some of these bars go dry, so even your ultra-light Hewes won't be floating across. These are not places you will want to stay overnight, so keep an eye on that tide.

The open waters of the harbor also have something to offer light-tackle anglers, because in fall there's often a mix of trout, jacks, ladyfish and Spanish mackerel running glass minnows in these otherwise barren depths. Finding the fish is a matter of finding diving birds or showering bait, and the best time to locate the action is early on a calm morning. Once you see the fish, casting a 1/4 ounce metal-flake swimmer-tail jig or a small chrome spoon will keep you busy. (Use 30-pound-test mono as a leader to prevent cutoffs by the mackerel.) One of the best trout guides in the area is Larry Lazoan of Port Charlotte, who still manages hundred-fish days with some regularity. Lazoan is also a noted tournament bass fisherman, and he catches all his fish on artificials--see the chapter on guides for his number.

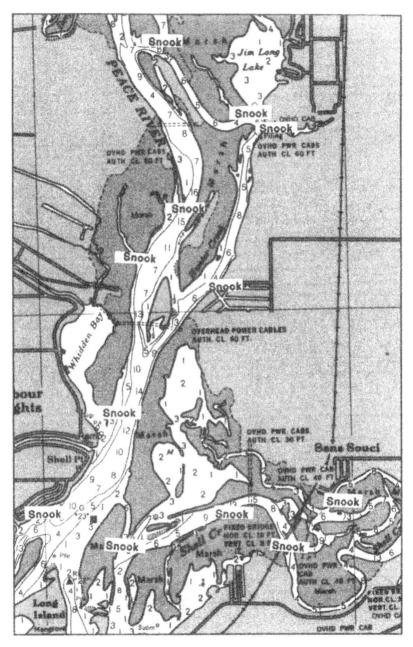

LOWER PEACE RIVER

CHAPTER 11

NORTHERN PINE ISLAND SOUND

The sound that stretches between Pine Island and the barrier islands of Cayo Costa, North Captiva, Captiva and Sanibel is unique, a broad, shallow area that has no freshwater rivers feeding into it to darken the water. But it gets a tremendous tidal flushing from the numerous passes, plus the giant mouth of Boca Grande on the north end and San Carlos on the south. It remains clear year around, has rich, undisturbed grass flats, and is loaded with fish. And, because of the numerous mangrove islands, there's always a place to fish out of the wind, no matter how bad the weather.

One stormy spring morning a few years ago, a friend and I fished there against better judgment in southwest winds that were blowing over 25 knots. Not only did we have no problems with rough seas, hiding in the basins and behind the mangrove islands on the northeast side of the sound, but we had one of the best topwater snook days either of us ever enjoyed.

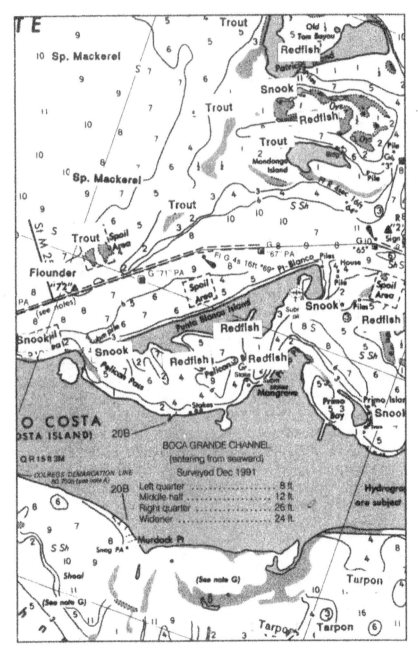

Cayo Costa/Punta Blanca Island

There was a rising tide, and with that wind behind it, it rose with a vengeance. In fact, the current created eddies and swirls where it boiled around the islands. Where ever there was one of those eddies, we soon figured out, there was a snook ready to blast a Bangolure.

Wild creatures learn to take advantage of whatever their environment gives them, and these snook had keyed on the tremendous tide flow, which was pushing loads of bait past the points. They were waiting in the eddies, out of the flow, much like rainbow trout in a mountain stream. When an edible floated by, they launched themselves on it.

We caught at least one fish on every point that cut the boiling tide at a right angle. The points on the north or south ends of the islands didn't produce, but those on the east and west ends were gold. Those that were particularly hot were the few with a "yellow hole" or slightly deeper, bald area backing up to the point--one of these spots produced a dozen strikes and four keeper-sized fish, amazing action for anglers not tossing live baits.

Interestingly, on the islands that ran north and south, the fish were scattered along the shoreline, rather than on the points. They were particularly likely to show up where the passages between islands necked down to a narrower section, which increased the effect of the tide flow.

One wacky 7-pounder came off an unnamed island north of Rocky Channel to strike at my lure five times, blasting it into the air repeatedly but missing the hook each time. On the last go round, about 20 feet from the boat, he caught the plug sideways in his mouth and snapped it in half! And they wonder why snook fishing is addictive. (This was in the days when Bangolures were made of soft wood, which would break on occasion. They have a tough piece of hardwood down the middle now, so they don't break anymore and cast farther, although some of us unreconstructed Bagleyites might insist that the old ones had a little quicker wobble and sometimes caught more fish. I still have three of 'em. Don't ask--I ain't selling.)

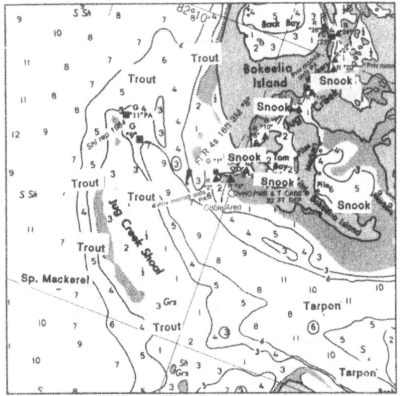

JUG CREEK SHOAL

Anyway, it was a wonderful morning and we probably didn't go 15 minutes without at least getting a boil (nice thing about fishing topwaters--you get to count the boils!) or a solid hit. By lunchtime the water had come in as far as it could, the flow stopped and so did the fishing. Then came the fun part, a ride home across the rather excited waters of Charlotte Harbor, but you can put up with some time in the saltwater firehose after a morning like that.

Pine Island Sound is about 15 miles long and 4 miles wide, and there's no place in it where the fishing is not good. In general, the patterns are much like those we found that morning for snook--find points and yellow holes with strong tide flows and you'll find the linesiders--and often reds and trout, too. However, remember that they won't be in all the spots that look likely-- you'll probably have to check a dozen or more before you find a live one, and some days you can look all day long until you hit that one hotspot. (OK, a few days you look all day long and DON'T hit that one hotspot. That's why they call it "fishing" instead of "catching".)

The flats action for snook begins in March and runs through November most years. There may be a slowdown around the new and full moons from May through July as many of the mature fish go to the passes to spawn, but in general the action is pretty steady throughout the warmer months. When the water temperature dips below 70 degrees, most of the snook will move, either heading to the offshore reefs in the Gulf or into deep canals and creeks of the back country.

JUG CREEK AND ITS SHOAL

Jug Creek is a saltwater creek that winds around the village of Bokeelia, on the northern tip of Pine Island. This is one of the few remaining spots around Charlotte Harbor where things are still somewhat like they were 20 years back, no traffic jams and no tourists in black socks and Bermuda shorts, though on weekends you will have to wait in line to have dinner in the Seafood Shack, which is a place well worth waiting to have dinner in. Rickety, old, and with wonderful eats, maybe the best boiled shrimp in Florida.

Jug Creek itself is generally murky from boat traffic--it's the only access to the small marinas of Bokeelia--but that doesn't prevent the snook from making use of its holes and channels. The west mouth is a good spot on falling tide, while the flat outside the east mouth can be good on the rise. On low water, the deeper areas are sometimes productive, and there are always fish around the docks in the marinas. (Bocilla Island Club has condos for rent just off the creek--it's a convenient place to stay, with an adjacent marina and within walking distance of the restaurant. A good thing about staying on the creek is that if the wind blows

You're likely to catch a bit of everything on Jug Creek Shoal, as this angler learned when a permit whacked his topwater lure. The species is usually a bottom-feeder that eats little more than crabs.

from the south or southwest, you go out the east mouth and fish down Matlacha Pass in protected water. If it blows from the north or northeast, you go out the west mouth and fish down Pine Island Sound, similarly in the lee.)

Jug Creek Shoal, outside the west mouth, is the northern terminus of the long flat that makes up Pine Island Sound. Beyond the shoal, the open waters of Charlotte Harbor fall away to 7-10 feet. On the shoal itself, however, the depth ranges from 1 to 4 feet, and because of the heavy flow of clear Gulf water with every rising tide, the turtle grass is particularly rich here, creating great trout habitat. This is the area where hook-and-line commercial trout fishermen used to make their days, trolling pigfish on a pair of long canepoles from small skiffs powered by inboard engines that ticked over at walking speed. There's still at least one of these fishermen left, and you'll see him out there, watching his poles from under a broad-brimmed straw hat, on occasion.

You might find trout anywhere along Jug Creek Shoal, but it sometimes takes a number of drifts in different areas to get on a school. The trick is to go in on the upwind side, keep the boat in about 3 feet and drift until you run out of grass or approach the mangrove shore. You then motor upwind and try another drift a hundred feet further on.

Noisy topwaters are the best trout locaters here, with propeller plugs like the 5M MirrOLure, Jerkin' Sam and Dalton Special

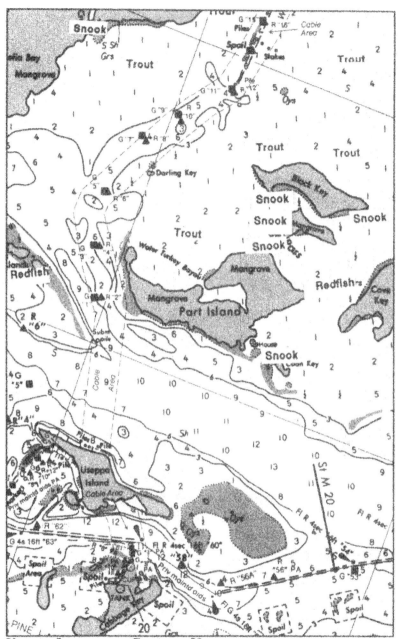

USEPPA ISLAND AND CABBAGE KEY

119

good for getting the fish to show themselves. Once you get a few boils and get a sense of where the school is located, you can sometimes catch more on the quieter floaters like the 7M, SP-5 Bango, Rapala and similars, plus slow-sinkers like the 52M, Rattlin' Flash or sinking Finger Mullet. Jigs and soft plastic jerkbaits are also very effective.

However, it seems to me that over the years I've caught more big trout, 4 pounds and up, on topwaters. But maybe that's because I throw the topwater more often when I'm in a likely spot. Anyway, it is definitely the essence of the sport to see a big yellow-mouth come up and inhale a floater with that distinctive "chug!" that trout make.

The shoal also attracts other stuff, redfish on the shallow edges, the occasional snook, and in spring and fall, Spanish mackerel and bluefish on the outside. A friend of mine even caught a permit in there once, on an SP-5 Bangolure floater, of all things.

There are two other shoals in this area, both small ones, but both productive. One lies due north of the Bokeelia Pier, about a half-mile out, the other is northeast of the eastern opening of Jug Creek, also about a half-mile out. If there's much wind blowing, you can forget these areas because they'll be too rough to fish, but on calm mornings they can produce wonderful topwater trout fishing. Both have shell and sand bars that go dry on extreme lows, but are surrounded by deep turtle grass and usually clear water. The west shoal, which is easily found due to channel markers 92 and 94 on its south edge, is surrounded by water over 12 feet deep and you might see anything including tarpon and cobia cruising by. The east shoal, which lies south of marker 87, has a deep grass basin on the inside, and that entire area is a good place to drift for trout.

ISLANDS IN THE SOUND

Useppa Island, near the north end of the Sound, is sort of a "forbidden island" for all but those who buy membership in the club there--only members and guests are allowed ashore. If you

You might find trout anywhere along Jug Creek Shoal, but it sometimes takes a number of drifts in different areas to get on a school.

can wangle an invitation, though, it's one of Florida's premiere hideaways, with quaint, 1920's cottages, half-million-dollar homes, swank condos and perhaps the nation's largest banyan tree. It was originally the domain of Barron Collier, one of Florida's founding fathers, but today is home to captains of industry, movie stars and others who simply "vant to be alone".

Cabbage Key, just a couple hundred yards across the ICW from Useppa, used to be the most pleasant anglers' hideaway in the state. Its rooms were (and are) rickety and old, it was home to countless billions of no-see-ums and mosquitoes, and its rustic bar and dollar-bill papered restaurant were secrets of only the cognoscenti of classic Florida.

Cayo Costa is all within a state park. It's nearly 6 miles long and up to a mile wide, and there are excellent campsites and rustic cabins for rent.

That's how it used to be, a great place to waste away, right in the middle of all the best snook and tarpon fishing. But, the wheel turns. Today, flocks of tourists arrive by tourboat hourly, and the lines extend out the restaurant door and almost down to the docks. Everybody wants their own piece of quaint, and that's the end of the Cabbage Key story, sad to say. (The fish don't mind the tourists--they still bite readily on the flats on the south side of the island.)

CAYO COSTA

Cayo Costa has escaped a similar fate because this incredibly valuable chunk of direct-gulf beachfront is all within a state park. It's nearly 6 miles long and up to a mile wide, and there are excellent campsites and rustic cabins for rent within a stone's throw of the ultra-clear Johnson Shoal basin. If you're overnighting, the safest thing to do is tie up at the docks on Pelican Bay, on the east side, and take the free tram or hike to the camping area. But, in calm summer weather the basin at Johnson Shoal makes an excellent, protected anchorage with fine swimming areas. The entry to the deep water is on the north end, where there's a 5-foot-deep channel--most of the time. The sands shift constantly, so you have to feel your way in.

From the campground, you can walk the beach up to Boca Grande Pass, where you'll catch some snook after dark on falling tides in spring. This area also gets a good March/April run of pompano, which will hit small white jigs or live sandfleas. And, if you've got big ideas, you can set out a whole mullet or bonito chunk on a 10/0 rig and probably tangle with some of the pass's famed jumbo sharks. If you hook up with one like Old Hitler, the alleged 17-foot hammerhead that ate tarpon here for years, expect an empty spool pronto. (You might also hook a tarpon fishing this way--they roam throughout the pass after dark.)

By day, you can stake out on the white sand of Johnson Shoal and expect to see plenty of tarpon moving in and out of the pass. When they're in the shallows, they'll take streamer flies and plugs readily. A couple years back, the fish moved onto Johnson by the thousands in late May and early June. It has been less predictable the last few seasons, but when conditions get just right, this area is tarpon soup.

On the east side of Cayo Costa is Punta Blanca Island, which has a deep channel cut around the south end. This can be productive on extreme low tides for snook and sometimes flounder. A grass flat begins south of Cabbage Key in this area, and extends for several miles south toward Captiva Pass. This flat frequently holds large schools of late summer and fall redfish. Pejuan Cove, which cuts into the south end of Cayo Costa, always has a few big reds along the deep mangrove shoreline. A spoon worked just outside the limbs will draw them out, as will the Love Lure Float-N-Jig, with a little noise-maker float to attract attention as you hop the jig.

PINELAND WATERS

Jumping back across the sound, Patricio Island has a deep, grassy channel along its north shore, and this can be a good topwater trout spot on strong tide flows. On the west side there's as much as 7 feet of water around the little oyster bars that separate Patricio from Mondongo Island, and on low water these cuts are worth a look--you may find snook there in summer, trout and reds in winter. A broad, deep channel separates Patricio from Little Bokeelia Island, and this area frequently holds big tarpon in late summer.

On extreme low tides, the Pineland Channel, which is marked, is a good spot for all flats species--it offers 6 feet of water cutting through shallows that are only a foot deep (and rocky, too, so don't try to run your outboard outside the marked water.)

The waters around Part Island are very shallow, but on all but the lowest tides flats rigs can operate in there, and there are lots of yellow holes attractive to snook. Check out the holes on the east side of Part and around Coon Key, on the south side. Also Wood Key and Little Wood Key are surrounded by holes that always hold a few snook, though these fish get picked over pretty heavily by resident anglers, most of whom fish live sardines.

In short, there's so much good water in the north end of Pine Island Sound that you can readily spend a week's fishing vacation there, and never run out of new water to fish. Yummy!

CHAPTER 12

SOUTHERN PINE ISLAND SOUND

The waters south of Captiva Shoal take on a different character from the northern end of the sound, with fewer islands, more deep water and somewhat narrower grass flats. However, the area still provides great fishing.

NORTH CAPTIVA

Captiva Shoal itself is a good place to start--the area where the waters of Captiva Pass first wash the flats is one of the prime spots in the sound to find live sardines, for those who know the magic these silvery baits work on snook. And, the sandy edges of these same flats provide great action on flounder in spring and fall.

Captiva Rocks, rocky shell bars just south of the old fishing shacks on the east side of the sound, are surrounded by fairly deep water, 4 to 6 feet, and this area is frequently a good trout producer in the fall and winter. A jig bounced along bottom is the

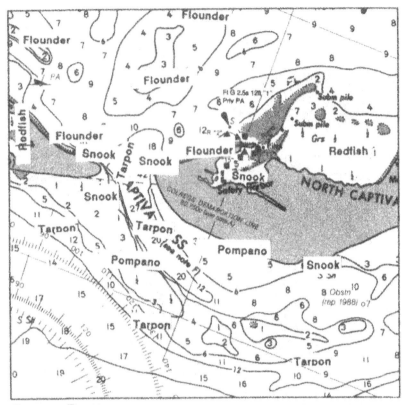

CAPTIVA PASS

most dependable offering, but slow-sinking plugs may catch larger fish. (Rocky Channel winds its way into the flats south of the shacks--it's a quick route to the shallows on low water, but it's challenging unless the sun is high and the water is clear. Miss a turn and you're in six inches of water, so go with caution.)

Pole east of the rocks into the shallows and you'll find a broad flat dotted with yellow holes, some of which hold snook, reds and trout spring through fall. The reds will be there pretty much all winter long, too. The waters south of Joselyn Island and north of Panther Key provide a protected basin where wind won't bother you unless there's a hard blow from the southwest, and even at that it won't get rough due to the shallow water. This is not an area to go blasting around in your shallow-draft rig if you don't know the bottom, though, because there are numerous very shallow areas (less than a foot deep at mid-tides) and also a fair number of areas that expose rock rather than sand bottom. Pole or use the trolling motor until you learn the water.

ISLAND HOPPING

Check the deep holes on the east side of Bird Key and the west side of Hemp Key on low water--both can be reached by deep channels that wind from the open sound back into foot-deep flats. Also, jigging the cuts around Demere Key can be productive. The flats meet the deeper water of the sound in a fairly well-defined edge from Demere south to MacKeever Keys, and this edge is worth a quick pass to check for reds pushing up on the flats with rising water. China Island, just west of MacKeever, has 10 feet of water right up to the shoreline and is sometimes a snook hotel. Check the channel mouth coming out of China on falling water. There's also a long, deep slough on the east side of MacKeever, which is a sometimes spot for trout and reds.

There are numerous shallow bayous down the east side of Sanibel island, but most of this water is too shallow to hold fish. However, the outlet channel of Sanibel Bayou has holes to 10 feet deep, and can be a killer spot on extreme low winter tides. The entrance is roughly due west of ICW marker 18.

Tarpon Bay is not a particularly good spot for tarpon any longer, but can be a fine spot for snook and reds. There's an oyster bar in the middle rising out of 5 feet of water that sometimes has reds willing to grab a spoon. The entry channel to Tarpon Bay has 9 feet of water, which makes it a good spot on the low end of a spring tide. The docks around Woodrings Point, at the mouth of the bay, can be good after dark for big snook.

CAPTIVA PASS

The pass also has an excellent run of snook in spring, May through July, as the fish gather there to spawn. The pods may show up anywhere along the bar, but are more often on the inside

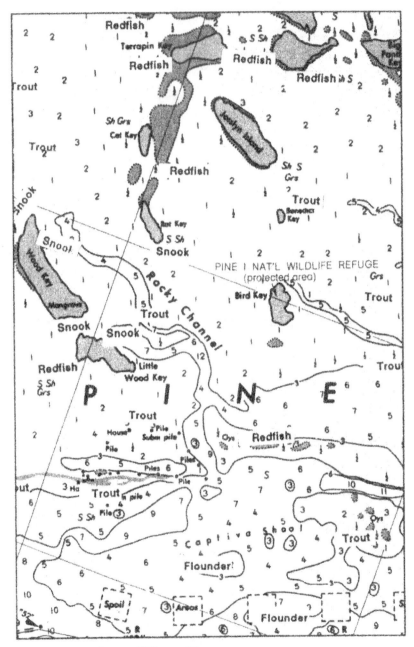

PINE ISLAND SOUND/WOOD KEY

corners than elsewhere. Some big ones are also caught along the slightly deeper slough that goes through the north bar just off the beach, though the action there is almost always after dark. Sardines are the ticket for fishing the main pass by day, but big plugs and 1/2 ounce jigs do the job after dark.

An odd problem occurs here due to the growing catch-and-release ethic of many anglers. Porpoises have learned that anytime a boat anchors inside the pass and begins pitching live sardines, there will soon be some tired snook swimming close by. The porpoises lie back about a hundred feet until the snook is boated, but when it is released it won't travel 20 feet before it goes down the gullet of Flipper. Some of the bigger porpoises have been known to eat three or four snook in a row, and technically there's nothing you can do about it, because they're protected from any form of harassment by the Marine Mammals Protection Law. (However, some of the local guides have learned that if you cast a 2-ounce jig close to the porpoises, they quickly get the message and head for other parts. Hey, officer, I was just trying to catch a tarpon!)

There are docks along the northeast tip of North Captiva Island, and these are noted spots for holding schools of linesiders in spring. It's usually necessary to fish live sardines or jumbo shrimp to get them, and heavy tackle is a must to pull them away from the cover. The docks that are lighted are excellent producers after dark, too, and often hold some big trout in fall, as well as the snook.

Captiva Pass is a midget compared to big brother Boca Grande, but it's 27 feet deep at its deepest point, moves lots of water, and at times holds plenty of tarpon in addition to the snook.

The tarpon can be caught in the same seasons and using the same methods that work for those in Boca Grande, by drifting the deep water with a squirrelfish, jumbo shrimp or crab fished near bottom on heavy gear. Alternatively, and far more interesting to most experienced anglers, you can wait for the fish to cruise out of the pass and cross the Captiva Bar, which extends about 2

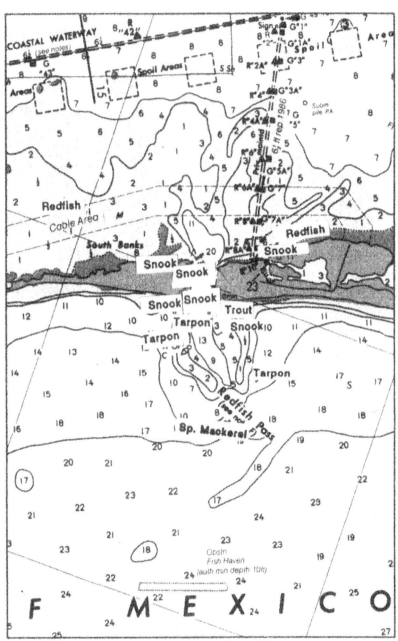

REDFISH PASS

miles to the southeast. The white sand bar, readily visible when the sun is high, ranges from 1 to 5 feet deep, and tarpon coming across it look like dark green torpedoes. They'll take flies, plugs or free-lined blue crabs.

Best way to make the offering is from a boat that's at rest, or being poled. The fish get plenty of pressure these days, and will definitely run away from boats that try to approach on outboard power. They're more tolerant of electric trolling motors, but even these seem to put them off after the first couple weeks of the season, which usually gets rolling about mid-May and continues to late July.

The fish seem to hang around the Captiva Shoal regularly, but also work along the beach with some frequency, apparently trading between here and Johnson Shoal, at the north end of Cayo Costa.

REDFISH PASS

Redfish Pass is famed not for reds, but for snook. Before the spawning season was closed to harvest, dozens of boats lined up here to drift the outgoing tide in June and July, and everybody caught fish.

These days, the snook are as abundant as ever, but few fish them because of the closed season--good news if you enjoy catch-and-release.

The fishing is much like tarpon fishing at Boca Grande. You sink a live shrimp, sardine or pinfish to bottom, which averages 15 to over 20 feet, and let it drift, easing the outboard into gear occasionally to keep the bait straight down. At the end of a swing through the deep water, you motor back to the inland side and repeat the drift.

You can also catch some of these fish by bumping a jig along bottom, although they generally won't take the artificial as readily as the live bait. You can catch plenty on artificials after dark, however. Casting from the beach at South Seas Plantation produces lots of fish after sundown--use a 1/2 ounce bucktail,

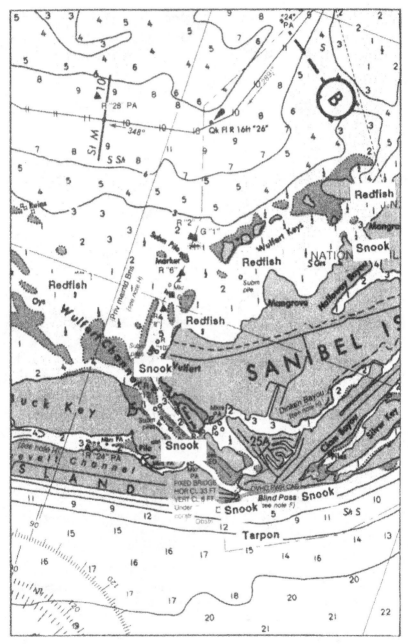

SANIBEL ISLAND/BLIND PASS

Brock Sargeant shows a hefty flounder that grabbed a tipped jig at the bar just inside Captiva Pass.

cast it upcurrent and let it sweep down, just ticking bottom as you retrieve. (Take plenty of jigs--there are lots of snags.)

Redfish Pass also gets a run of big trout in spring, April or May, and these fish are likely to gather around the rock groins on the south side and along the south bar, where they'll take jigs and topwaters early and late. There are snook around those rocks all summer long, as well.

Inside the pass, southeast of the entry channel to South Seas Marina, there's a shallow grass flat that runs for hundreds of yards along the mangroves. This flat is locally famous as a producer of big snook, reds and trout that come up out of the pass to feed on high tides. Free-lined sardines are the surest bait, but topwaters also get them. The water is clear and shallow, and it's pretty much essential to wade to avoid spooking the fish. The best action is when the highs come at dawn, dusk or after dark--

take mosquito repellent and Skin So Soft to protect against no-see-ums.

CAPTIVA AND SANIBEL

These two islands used to be angling heaven, perfectly located in the heart of some of Florida's finest waters, isolated, quiet and so breath-takingly beautiful. They had a few fish camps, basic, cheap and run by folks who knew what inshore angling was about.

But, progress conquers all--today, Sanibel is about as attractive as downtown Tampa at rush hour. Captiva, though better, requires a long, 30-mph crawl to access, and the narrow road is always loaded with traffic. You can forget the delightful little fish camps, too--the few that still survive now cater to the winter tourists, at prices of $100 per day and up.

If you can afford it, South Seas Plantation is without question the premiere spot to stay here, with marina villas only a few steps from the docks and also within walking distance of Redfish Pass for a bit of night snooking. 'Tween Waters Inn, a few miles south on Captiva, still welcomes anglers, though at considerably higher prices than in the old days. Unfortunately, all the folks who own the accommodations have realized that yacht owners, golfers and tennis players spend lots of money in their gift shops, eat dinner in their expensive restaurants and make them rich. Fishermen, on the other hand, steal ice out of the ice machines, wake up the other customers at 5 a.m. as they drag tackle through the halls, and eat baloney sandwiches in the boat. They don't go for our sort of rough trade down there any more. Sigh.

That said, the fishing is still very good around these islands. The waters around Blind Pass--which separates Captiva from Sanibel--are particularly good to explore for snook. Find areas where the old channel sweeps in close to the shore and fish the docks early and late. The pass itself has some jumbo snook in late spring and summer, and the south beach is a good place to wade-fish after dark at this time, tossing a 52-M on outgoing tide. Roosevelt Channel, which makes off to the north behind Buck

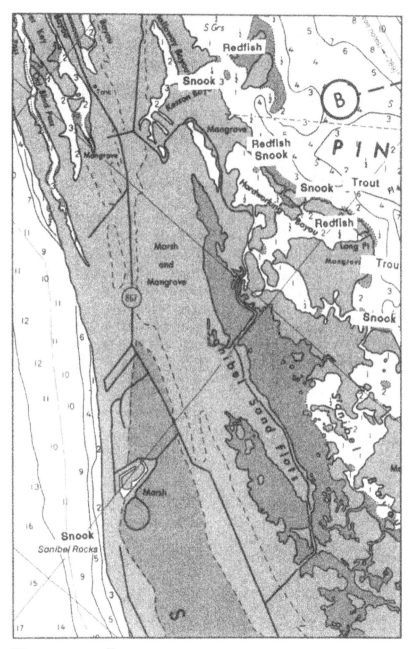

HARDWORKING BAYOU

Key from Blind Pass, has 7 foot depths and lots of docks, and can be a good after-dark spot for snook.

CANAL FISHING

There are several man-made canals on the southern half of Pine Island, and in winter these deep channels offer temperature refuges to cold-sensitive species. The canals are located south of Demere Key, north of Mason Island, and in the town of St. James City, on the southern tip of the island. When fishing gets tough or impossible on the flats, these areas are always worth a look for those with small boats and trolling motors.

Monroe Canal, the largest at St. James City, extends inland over a mile, with numerous side canals winding away from it. Though it lacks the esthetics of fishing untouched mangrove country, the waters hold snook, trout, reds and jacks all winter long. (For keeper snook, visit this area a day or two after the first really cold weather of the year sweeps through, usually in late November or early December. Within a few weeks after the surge most of the keepers have been caught and kept, and only smaller snook remain.)

CHAPTER 13

MATLACHA PASS AND SAN CARLOS BAY

San Carlos Bay is sort of an extension of Matlacha Pass--or vice versa. In any case, there's a whole lot of gulf water flowing in and out of this area, plus a unique combination of very deep water right next to very shallow flats. As with most areas, this "edge" in habitat creates a great feeding spot for a wide variety of fish, and you might tangle with anything from flounder to king mackerel on a given day, all without traveling more than three miles from the boat ramp at the foot of the Sanibel Bridge.

YORK ISLAND

The waters west of York Island are interesting because there are shoals here to as little as a foot of water, almost within casting distance of 20-foot channels. The edges, indicated by the markers of the Intracoastal Waterway, are good spots for flounder if you fish live killifish or sardines, or bounce jigs down the incline. You'll also see Spanish mackerel running up into this

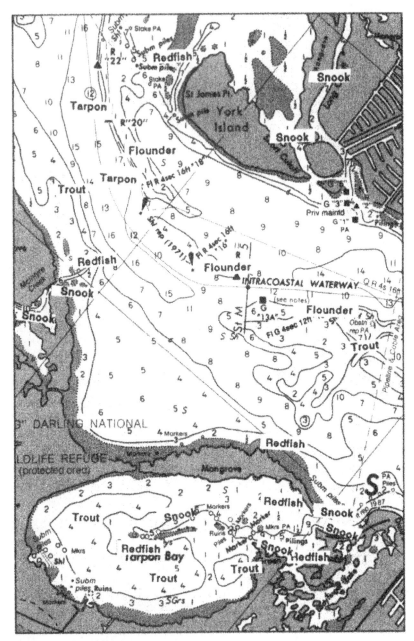

TARPON BAY/YORK ISLAND

Shallow-draft flats rigs are now the standard boat throughout the southwest coast. Most anglers use a trolling motor to approach their hotspots, then move into casting range on the pushpole to assure silence.

area and around Woodrings Point, due south, at times in spring and fall, and if you set up on the edges of the shoal and chum with fresh-ground sardines, you'll draw some nice ones into range. You may see a cobia cruising by from April through June, as well.

SAN CARLOS BAY

This same sort of action is even better as you approach the open waters of San Carlos Bay, both on the west point, Point Ybel, and the east point, Punta Rassa. On both points, there's 20 feet of water on a vertical drop from wading depths, and a bit of everything from both inside and outside waters shows up at various times of the year.

There are three bridges in the causeway leading to Sanibel Island, and any one of the spans may produce tarpon or cobia throughout the warmer months. However, the deeper water is under the eastern span, where there's as much as 22 feet in the

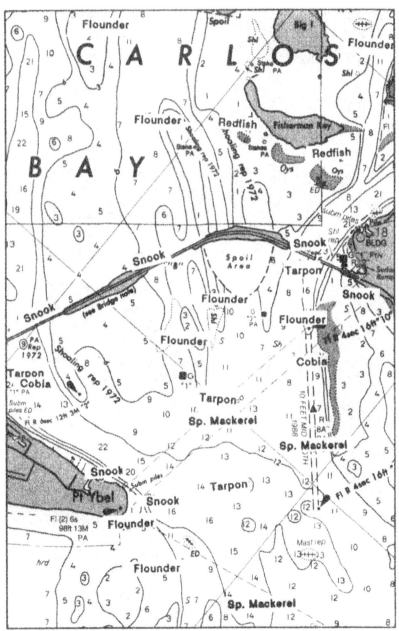

SAN CARLOS BAY

channel. The center span has lesser depths, about 8 feet, and the western span is more open water with depths of about 18 feet-- a popular spot for anglers to anchor and put out live baits, cut mullet or shad for tarpon.

There's a long, submerged point extending southwest from Punta Rassa and the foot of the Sanibel Bridge, and the tip of this point is a good spot to set up and chum for Spanish and even king mackerel. Chum with fresh-cut sardines and fish with free-lined sardines for the most dependable action. (You might catch a tarpon or cobia doing the same thing.)

Punta Rassa Cove, with the entry just north of the bridge, collects a variety of reds, snook and trout at times. It's very shallow on low, but deep enough on mid- to high tides. There are some deep holes in the back or south part of this bay that sometimes hold fish in winter. Work the southwest slough coming out of the cove on falling water for snook.

THE CALOOSAHATCHEE RIVER

Cattle Dock Point, which is just inside the mouth of the Caloosahatchee River, has 15 feet of water in tight to the shore, and opens via a narrow channel into Glover Bight, which is as much as 17 feet deep. This can be a good area for big trout in winter--bounce a quarter-ounce plastic-tailed jig down the edges of the drop. You may catch silver trout in this hole, as well. Slow-troll a jig just off bottom to find them. Follow the channel in tight to shore to the north and enter the canal, and you're in a maze of cuts where winter snook are regular visitors. Look particularly for areas where the deep water meets shallower outlets--good spots on falling water. Also check corners, where snook like to trap baits. If you're patient and willing to wait for a big fish, drift these deep canals with a live, 8-inch mullet just off bottom.

The Caloosahatchee River holds lots of tarpon in late summer, and is a snook highway in winter. The hot water outflow from the electrical powerplant is a noted hotspot for snook, trout and small tarpon in winter. Live shrimp is a sure thing, but plastic-

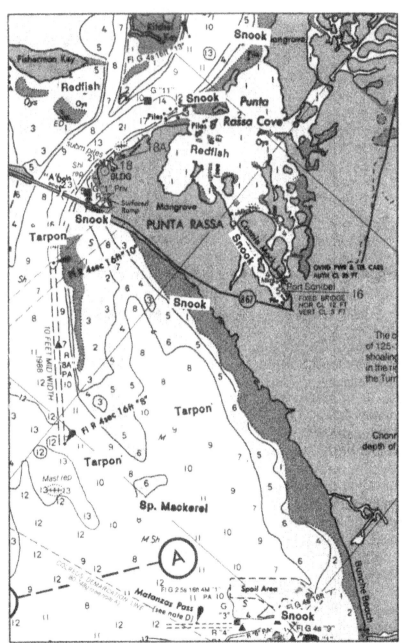

PUNTA RASSA

tailed jigs also do lots of business. With either, best action is via pitching the offering up-current and sweeping it back along bottom. You'll also catch more big jacks than you want with this technique, plus an occasional whopper trout.

Snook make their way all the way to Lake Okeechobee through the Caloosahatchee, but fishing is best in the stretches from the powerplant seaward. Tarpon also go well upriver, and you can occasionally jump them there in late summer on sinking plugs.

MATLACHA PASS

The town of Matlacha is an anachronism, one of those wonderful little fishing hideaways that the wave of development has somehow passed over. There are still mom-and-pop motels here that cater to fishermen, baitshops that are open when you want them to be, and a remarkably easy access to prime fishing in the back country. There's not much town to it, mostly just the little businesses that survive astraddle the Pine Island Bridge, but for anglers there's enough.

Matlacha is more of a saltwater river than a pass. It's nearly 12 miles from Bokeelia, on the north end, to St. James City, on the south--a whole lot longer than the passes we speak of conventionally in Florida. The river splits to flow around little Pine Island, but the vast majority of the water flows through the broader channel on the east side. The water is dark most of the time, stained by the tannin pouring out of the Peace and Myakka Rivers farther up Charlotte Harbor as well as from the mangrove creeks, but it's still highly productive.

Matlacha Pass begins roughly about Marker 81 on the north end, and just southwest of this marker is a long, narrow shell bar with water about 3 feet deep on the bay side. This bar has a unique attraction for big reds--it nearly always holds a fish or two in the 12- to 15-pound class from spring through late fall. A gold spoon or a topwater plug will get their attention. It's best to get out of the boat and wade the bar, since the water here is usually clear.

a winter moon tide. (Tucked in against the north shore, too, so those howling winter winds can't bother you.)

South of Sword Point, where the Caloosahatchee makes a 90-degree bend to head out into San Carlos Bay, there are a number of deep holes, up to 13 feet, that sometimes attract snook in spring and summer. The trick is to anchor on the bars, which are only a couple of feet deep, and wade the edges, casting to the deeper water with 1/2 ounce jigs. If the fish are there, they're most likely to bite on strong outgoing tides.

CHAPTER 14

ESTERO BAY TO NAPLES

Estero Bay and the adjoining smaller bays, including Hurricane Bay, Hell Peckney Bay, Big Hickory Bay, Fish Trap Bay and Little Hickory Bay, are little-known outside the Fort Myers area, but the abundance of shallow flats, shell bars, tidal creeks and gulf passes makes for fine inshore fishing here. And, much of it can be fished despite unfavorable wind conditions due to the abundant mangrove islands.

MATANZAS PASS

Matanzas Pass curls around the north end of Estero Island, on which Fort Myers Beach is located. The pass drains not only Estero Bay, but also the smaller Hell Peckney and Hurricane bays. Much of the length of the pass is heavily developed, which makes it esthetically unappealing, but all those docks, bridges and dredged channels make the snook very happy, thank you.

The north entry to Hurricane Bay, which is well-marked, makes off the main pass channel just inside the tip of Estero Island. Follow it inside to Marker 13 and you'll see residential

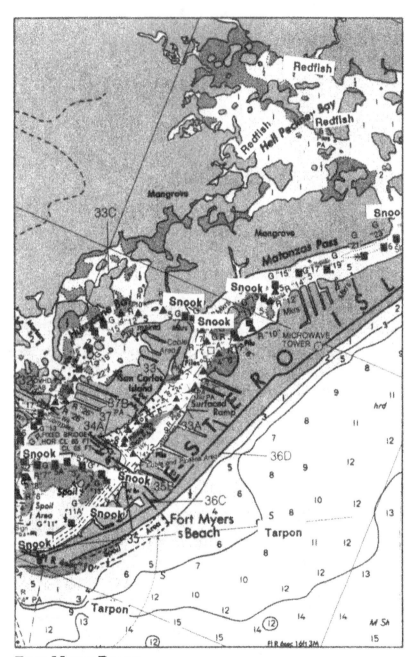

FORT MYERS BEACH

canals going off to the north. These canals have 8 feet of water at low tide, and can be good winter spots for snook, and sometimes for reds and trout. On the south entry to Hurricane Bay, there's a little tidal creek entering about Marker 6, on the east shore, that can be worth fishing on falling water for snook. There are also some bruisers that hang around the main Fort Myers Beach bridge, but catching them is primarily an after-dark, live-bait proposition--leave your 4-pound-test at home.

ESTERO BAY

This bay, about 5 miles long and 2 miles wide, is fed by a series of darkwater creeks, including Hendry Creek, Mullock Creek, the Estero River and Spring Creek. The influx of fresh water makes it prime estuary country. Hendry Creek is the largest of the flowages, and has the best depth, with up to 7 feet at the mouth around Dixon Point. There are numerous shallow bars upriver, but also more deep water--it's worth exploring on a trolling motor for snook. Mullock Creek is much narrower, but has some interesting branches and bars near the mouth, likely areas for reds in late summer. Hendry, Mullock and the Estero River all flow into a section aptly named Rocky Bay, which is loaded with oyster bars, unmarked rocks--and redfish. A spoon worked around the bars will do some business pretty much year around, and you may catch some big trout in there in spring on the same lure or a topwater. (Don't assume you're clear of the bars when you get away from the shoreline--some of them pop up a mile from shore.)

BIG CARLOS AND NEW PASSES

Big Carlos doglegs south around the beach at Lover's Key, and this area is likely for spawning snook in summer. Live sardines are the best bet due to the clear water--cruise just off the drop and look for pods of fish, or drift a crippled sardine down the tide and watch for busting fish to locate them. The bridge from Carlos Point to Black Island is also prime holding water from spring through late fall--good water for a night-time lunker

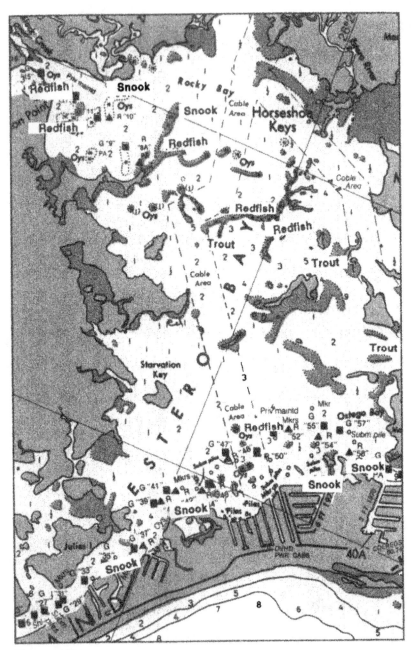

ESTERO BAY

Nighttime around the passes is a peaceful and productive time for snook.

on a big pigfish, live mullet or small ladyfish. Also, there's a slough making off from the pass to the north, in close to the beach, where snook sometimes pod up after sundown and will take a big diving plug or topwater.

There's a basin inside the pass to the north where snook and trout sometimes gather in winter. It's just west of Marker 66, reached via a narrow channel that opens out into a larger harbor with depths of 12 feet.

The bar at Big Carlos extends more than a half-mile from the beach, and the outer edges of this bar are a good place to check

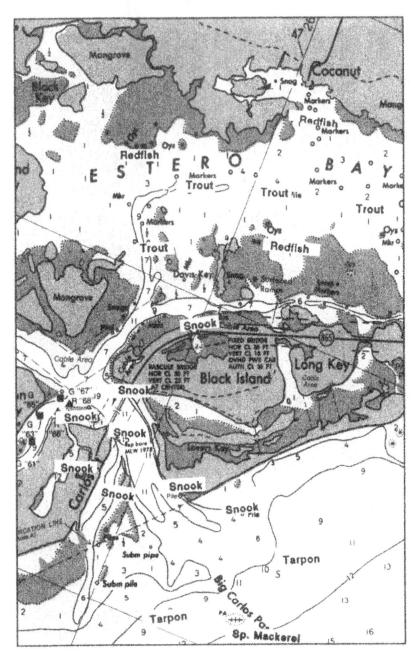

BIG CARLOS PASS

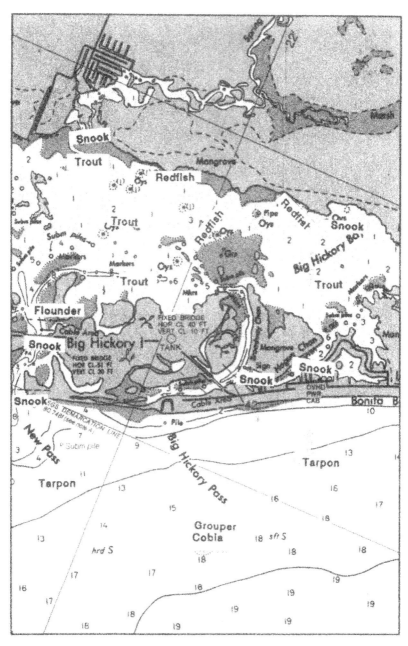

NEW PASS/BIG HICKORY BAY

153

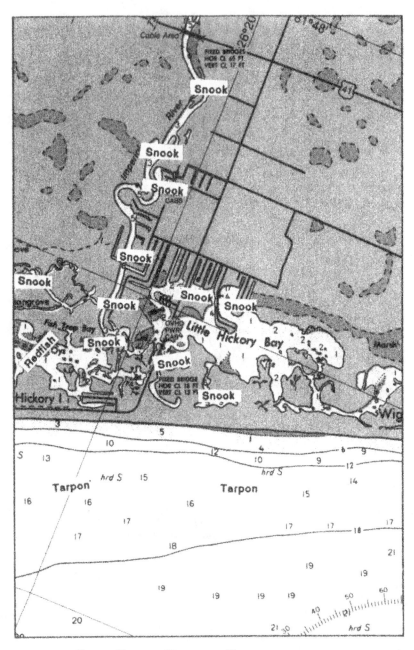

IMPERIAL RIVER/LITTLE HICKORY BAY

for tarpon on summer mornings. The water is usually clear, and they'll take flies and plugs as well as live baits.

Big Carlos splits just inside the bridge, and then the south leg splits again to flow around both sides of Davis Key. The eastern leg of the pass, about 7 feet deep, wanders off into the shallows of Estero Bay, where the water is scarcely a foot deep. The flats near this cut are good for reds on high water, while the edges of the channel are good for flounder on the drop. At the lower end of a big moon tide, you may find a bit of everything in the channel, where you can tap the action with a 1/4 ounce jig bounced along bottom. Add a small tip of shrimp or Pro Bait on days when the catfish are not excessively abundant.

New Pass is much narrower and shallower (maximum about 8 feet) than Big Carlos, but it can also hold spawner snook in spring, particularly around the tip of Big Hickory Island on the south side. The bridge also produces snook after dark. New Pass doglegs south like Big Carlos, and like Big Carlos, this narrow but deep channel--9 feet surrounded by foot-deep flats, is a good spot on the bottom end of low tides. Spring Creek flows into the east side of Estero Bay here, and the fresh water has grown lots of oysters in the flats--good places to pole or wade as you cast a spoon for reds.

BIG HICKORY BAY TO WIGGINS PASS

Big Hickory Bay is not really all that big, only about a mile square, but it's big compared to Little Hickory Bay to the south, which is only about a half-mile wide. There's been a good bit of dredging and development in the area, with lots of residential canals offering deep water. The Imperial River flows into Fish Trap Bay here, which lies between the two Hickory bays, and it's a substantial river in the lower reaches, with average depth of over 5 feet. Points, bars and creek outfalls are all likely places to find winter snook in the Imperial. The narrow, winding creeks that make off to the north out of the lower Imperial have some deep holes, and these are good spots to hit on falling water for snook and reds.

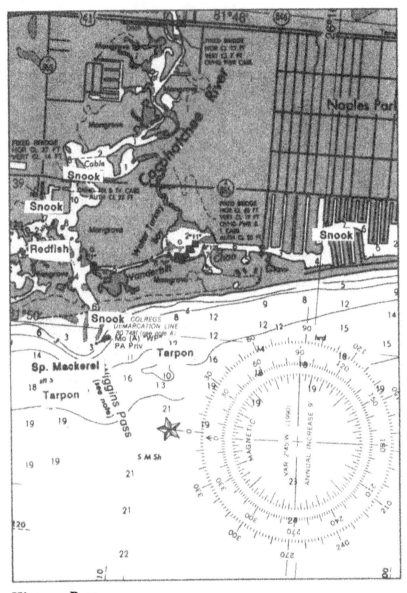

WIGGINS PASS

Big trout can be found from Estero Bay to Naples in the spring.

Wiggins Pass is a minor pass compared to many others along the southwest coast, but it still moves a fair amount of water, and on summer mornings you can often tangle with snook on either side of the bar and along the nearby beaches. Wiggins is the outfall for the Cocohatchee River, not a big flowage by any means, but it has some 10-foot water on the inside around the State Route 865 bridge, and holds some big snook year around.

Vanderbilt Channel makes off from Wiggins to the south, and it opens into Naples Park Basin, where there are lots of docks extending into 6 feet of water. There's not a lot of tide flow in this basin so the water quality goes up and down, but when it's right there can be good numbers of fish in there.

From Wiggins southward to Naples, the beach is frequently productive for snook due to rock groins, as well as bars built up by now-closed passes. You'll also find tarpon cruising from 100 yards to a half-mile off the beach throughout the summer.

CHAPTER 15

NAPLES TO MARCO

The last two cities on the southwest coast of Florida have a largely tropical climate where the seasonal variations in fishing are not nearly so pronounced as further north. The region is prime country for tarpon, and regularly produces some of the biggest snook caught in Florida each year. The usual seasonal migrations of the inshore pelagics, kings, Spanish and cobia, are at their best a month or more earlier than in the rest of the peninsula here, and grouper fishing remains good throughout the winter.

NAPLES BAY AND GORDON PASS

Though highly developed, the waters here are noted for consistent production of lunker snook and occasional giant redfish, as well--some fish of both species in the 40-pound-class have been taken by railbirds at the Naples Municipal Pier.

Naples Bay is created by the outflow of the Gordon River, Rock Creek and Haldeman Creek. The entire town of Naples is riddled with dredged canals, and you might find snook down

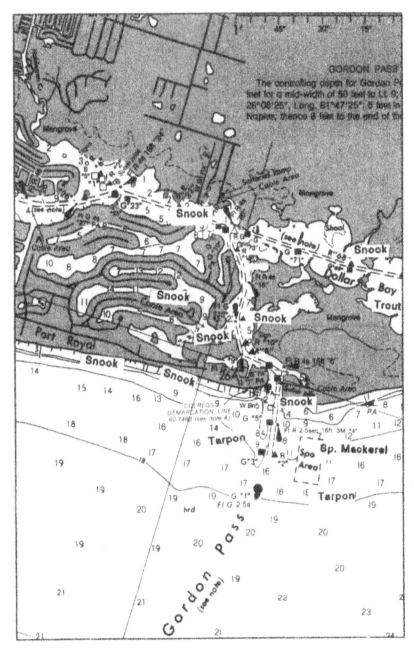

GORDON PASS/NAPLES

Tarpon are abundant in the Marco area throughout the warmer months, with lots of big ones along the beaches, smaller fish in the big jungle rivers.

virtually any one of these cuts. However, the most certain are those larger canals near Gordon Pass. The cuts there are 10 to 14 feet deep and much broader than most dug canals, and consequently offer more habitat for big fish. The single entrance to reach three of these major canals is just inside Marker 10, and makes off to the north.

Between Doctor's Pass and Gordon Pass, the beaches are loaded with groins to prevent erosion, and these are excellent locations to find snook from May through October. Best action is usually on summer mornings, before the sea breeze begins to roil the water. The fish will be found up tight against the rocks, so don't make the tourist's mistake of casting as far into the gulf as possible--often a cast parallel to the sand and just 10 feet from the beach is the one that connects. (Due to the usually-clear water, this is a good place to fish a realistic-looking artificial like the DOA Baitrunner, a plastic finger mullet imitation.)

Tarpon often hang around the north bar at Gordon's Pass, and around the spoil area to the south. That spoil area is also a good place to anchor and chum with ground fish for Spanish mackerel and kings.

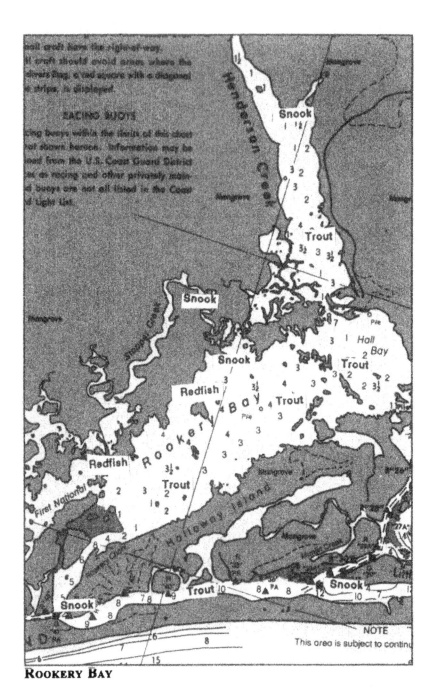

ROOKERY BAY

Rookery Bay is a significant habitat break, because it's the first outpost of the 10,000 Islands and the Everglades beyond, the vast wilderness that makes up the entire southern tip of the state.

The north point of Halloway Island, at ICW marker 47, is a good place to soak a big live bait for snook and reds on outgoing tide. Rookery Channel feeds into the ICW here. Follow that channel back into Rookery Bay and you'll see many small mangrove creeks and islands to the east. This shoreline is usually host to redfish and the occasional snook, while the open water of the bay, averaging 3 to 4 feet, holds trout in spring and fall. There's a deep hole where Henderson Creek feeds into the bay, and this is a good spot for live sardines on the bottom half of the tide.

Big Marco River winds off through the islands toward Goodland and the 10,000 Islands beyond, and most of the length of this broad, deep flow is good for tarpon. Snook are always a good bet where smaller creeks fall into the river, and around the numerous dredged residential canals of Marco Island. Fish the points in Addison Bay and Unknown Bay for snook, and hit the mangrove shorelines on high tides for reds--a popping cork with a jig or shrimp pulls them out of the cover.

There's an amazing selection of passes in the Marco area, all of them productive from May through August. Hurricane and Little Marco exit at Cannon Island, just north of Marco. Both are shallow as passes go, but drifting and chumming with sardines will often cause pods of fish to reveal their location here. Capri Pass and Big Marco Pass, which are the main outfalls of the Big Marco River, make up a jumbo pass with water as much as 32 feet deep, a tarpon highway, and an excellent area for really huge snook. Check the outlet from the Isles of Capri, Cannon Channel, and the cut that goes into Collier Bay, plus the north Marco bridge. The waters around Coconut Island were the historic location where fishing for spawning snook got started decades ago, and at one time attracted fleets of boats--so many, in fact,

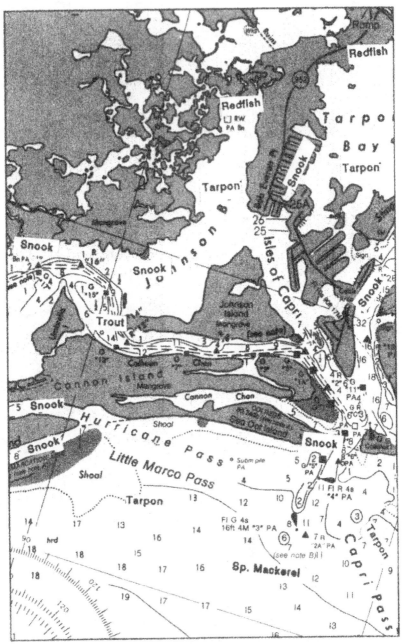

LITTLE MARCO/HURRICANE/CAPRI PASSES

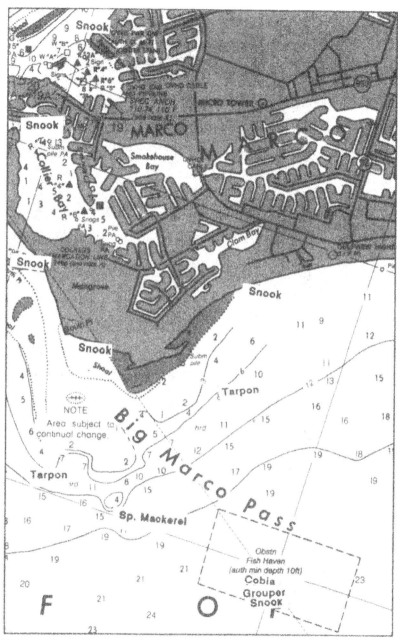

MARCO ISLAND AND BIG MARCO PASS

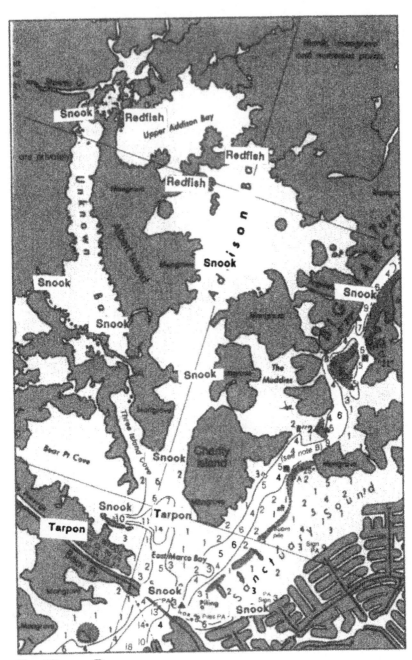

BIG MARCO RIVER

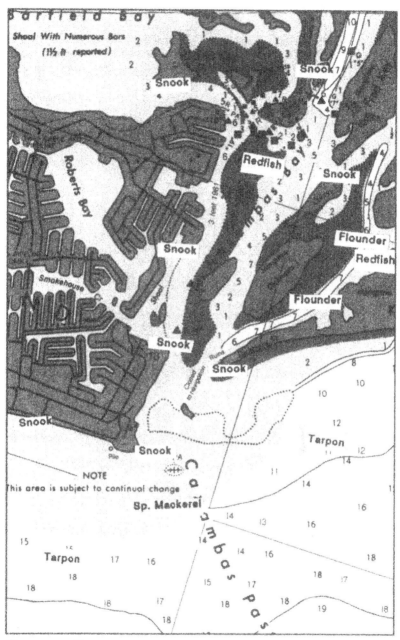

CAXAMBAS PASS

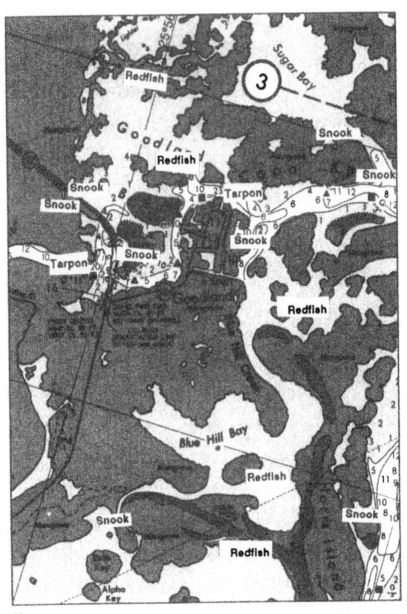

GOODLAND

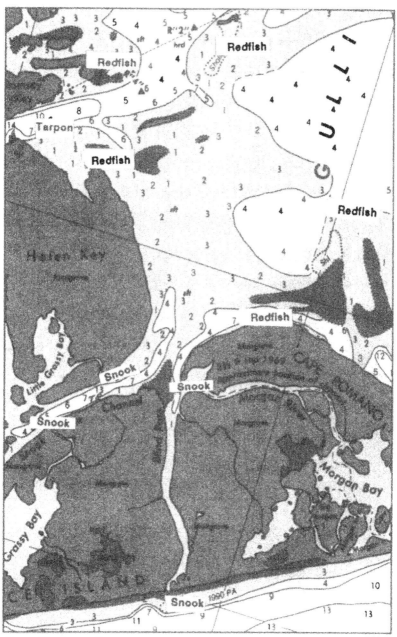

CAPE ROMANO ISLAND

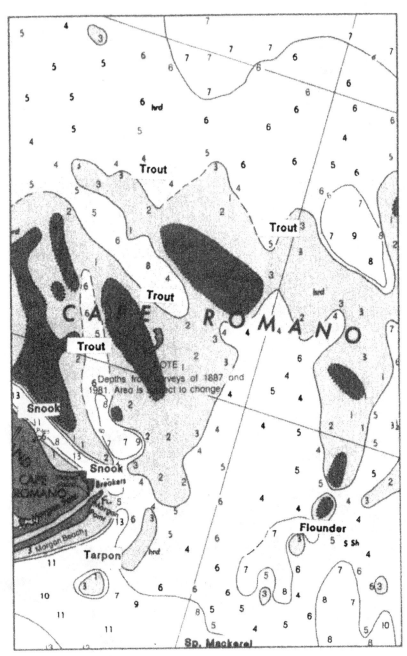

CAPE ROMANO SHOALS

that they knocked the snook population out. Declining catches here and at Naples were the factors that brought on the closed summer season, which we have to thank for the remarkable snook restoration.

Caxambas Pass empties Caxambas, Roberts and Barfield bays, and often holds fish right against the beach in late summer. Also worth checking is the 7-foot channel that swings southeast around Dickman's Point. And finally, check out the Cape Romano channel, which runs right along the beach of Cape Romano Island, the last inhabited island of the west coast barrier island chain. The water in this cut is as much as 13 feet deep, but Cape Romano Shoal rises to only a foot deep just beyond it. The cut itself often holds fish, sometimes right against the beach, as do some of the deep holes scattered here and there across the cape shoals.

Beyond Cape Romano, the 10,000 Islands beckon with endless fishing opportunities, all of them easily reached from lodging here or at Port of the Islands, east on U.S. 41, but we'll save that for another time.

CHAPTER 16

GUIDES

Fishing opportunities along the southwest coast of Florida varies from big open bays that anyone with a seaworthy boat can manage to intricate shallows loaded with rocks guaranteed to snag the unwary. Finding your way around some of the better areas takes either long experience or the services of a good local guide. The following list is by no means all-inclusive, but it's a good start on the prime areas. Local marinas and the yellow pages of the telephone book in the area you want to fish can also connect you with the pros.

Babe Darna, Boca Grande (813) 964-2559
Ray DeMarco, Anna Maria (813) 778-9215
Dave Eimers, Pine Island (813) 353-4828
Freddy Futch, Boca Grande (813) 964-2266
Ad Gilbert, Venice, (813) 484-8430
Pete Greenan, Charlotte Harbor (813) 923-6095
Paul Hawkins, St. Petersburg (813) 894-7345
Jeff Hilliard, Sarasota Bay, (813) 776-2308
Van Hubbard, Boca Grande (813) 697-6944

Cappy Joiner, Boca Grande (813) 697-6052
Lamar Joiner, Boca Grande (813) 697-4939
Larry Lazoan, Port Charlotte, (813) 627-1704
Tim McOsker, Boca Grande (813) 475-5908
Larry Mendez, Charollotte Harbor (813) 874-3474
Bill Miller, Charlotte Harbor (813) 935-3141
Chris Mitchell, Boca Grande (813) 964-2887
Scott Moore, Cortez/Boca Grande (813) 778-3005
Brian Mowatt, Charlotte Harbor, (813) 624-4920
Jim Nickerson, Naples, (813) 353-5448
Phil O'Bannon, Fort Myers, (813) 964-0359
Jay Peeler, Marco, (813) 642-1342
Glenn Puopolo, Naples, (813) 353-4807
Pete Villani, Naples, (813) 262-8228
Jim Wisner, Tampa Bay, (813) 831-5659
Phil Woods, Boca Grande, (813) 964-2393
Jon Zorian, Boca Grande, (813) 964-2038

As a final note, the Boca Grande Guides Association, at Boca Grande Pass, publishes an excellent how-to brochure on fishing the pass, with a complete list of guides' phone numbers. Send a self-addressed, stamped envelope to P.O. Box 676, Boca Grande, FL 33921.

175

BASS SERIES LIBRARY
by Larry Larsen

(BSL1) FOLLOW THE FORAGE - BASS/PREY RELATIONSHIP - Learn how to determine dominant forage in a body of water and catch more bass!

(BSL2) VOL. 2 BETTER BASS ANGLING TECHNIQUES - Learn why one lure or bait is more successful than others and how to use each lure under varying conditions.

(BSL3) BASS PRO STRATEGIES - Professional fishermen know how changes in pH, water level, temperature and color affect bass fishing, and they know how to adapt to weather and topographical variations. Learn from their experience.

(BSL4) BASS LURES - TRICKS & TECHNIQUES - When bass become accustomed to the same artificials and presentations seen over and over again, they become harder to catch. You will learn how to modify your lures and rigs and how to develop new presentation and retrieve methods to spark the interest of largemouth!

(BSL5) SHALLOW WATER BASS - Bass spend 90% of their time in waters less than 15 feet deep. Learn productive new tactics that you can apply in marshes, estuaries, reservoirs, lakes, creeks and small ponds, and you'll triple your results!

(BSL6) BASS FISHING FACTS - Learn why and how bass behave during pre- and post-spawn, how they utilize their senses when active and how they respond to their environment, and you'll increase your bass angling success!

(BSL7) TROPHY BASS - If you're more interested in wrestling with one or two monster largemouth than with a "panful" of yearlings, then learn what techniques and locations will improve your chances.

(BSL8) ANGLER'S GUIDE TO BASS PATTERNS - Catch bass every time out by learning how to develop a productive pattern quickly and effectively. "Bass Patterns" is a reference source for all anglers, regardless of where they live or their skill level. Learn how to choose the right lure, presentation and habitat under various weather and environmental conditions!

(BSL9) BASS GUIDE TIPS - Learn secret techniques known only in a certain region or state that often work in waters all around the country. It's this new approach that usually results in excellent bass angling success. Learn how to apply what the country's top guides know!

Nine Great Volumes To Help You Catch More and Larger Bass!

(LB1) LARRY LARSEN ON BASS TACTICS

is the ultimate "how-to" book that focuses on proven productive methods. **Hundreds of highlighted tips and drawings in our LARSEN ON BASS SERIES explain how you**

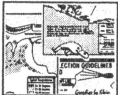

can catch more and larger bass in waters all around the country. This reference source by America's best known bass fishing writer will be invaluable to both the avid novice and expert angler!

(PF1) PEACOCK BASS EXPLOSIONS! by Larry Larsen

A must read for those anglers who are interested in catching the world's most exciting fresh water fish! Detailed tips, trip planning and tactics for peacocks in South Florida, Venezuela, Brazil, Puerto Rico, Hawaii and other destinations. This book explores the most effective tactics to take the aggressive peacock bass. You'll learn how to catch

more and larger fish using the valuable information from the author and expert angler, a four-time peacock bass world-record holder. It's the first comprehensive discussion on this wild and colorful fish.

BASS WATERS GUIDE SERIES by Larry Larsen

The most productive bass waters are described in this multi-volume series, including boat ramps, seasonal tactics, water characteristics and more. Numerous maps and photos detail specific locations.

(BW1) GUIDE TO NORTH FLORIDA BASS WATERS - Covers from Orange Lake north and west. Includes Lakes Lochloosa, Talquin and Seminole, the St. Johns, Nassau, Suwannee and Apalachicola Rivers; Newnans Lake, St. Mary's River, Juniper Lake, Ortega River, Lake Jackson, Deer Point Lake, Panhandle Mill Ponds and many more!

(BW2) GUIDE TO CENTRAL FLORIDA BASS WATERS - Covers from Tampa/Orlando to Palatka. Includes Lakes George, Rodman, Monroe, Tarpon and the Harris Chain, the St. Johns, Oklawaha and Withlacoochee Rivers, the Ocala Forest, Crystal River, Hillsborough River, Conway Chain, Homosassa River,

Lake Minneola, Lake Weir, Lake Hart, Spring Runs and many more!

(BW3) GUIDE TO SOUTH FLORIDA BASS WATERS - Covers from I-4 to the Everglades. Includes Lakes Tohopekaliga, Kissimmee, Okeechobee, Poinsett, Tenoroc and Blue Cypress, the Winter Haven Chain, Fellsmere Farm 13, Caloosahatchee River, Lake June-in-Winter, the Everglades, Lake Istokpoga, Peace River, Crooked Lake, Lake Osborne, St. Lucie Canal, Shell Creek, Lake Marian, Lake Pierce, Webb Lake and many more!

OUTDOOR TRAVEL SERIES
by Larry Larsen and M. Timothy O'Keefe

Candid guides on the best charters, time of the year, and other recommendations that can make your next fishing and/or diving trip much more enjoyable.

(OT1) FISH & DIVE THE CARIBBEAN - Vol. 1 Northern Caribbean, including Cozumel, Cayman Islands, Bahamas, Jamaica, Virgin Islands. Required reading for fishing and diving enthusiasts who want to know the most cost-effective means to enjoy these and other Caribbean islands.

(OT3) FISH & DIVE FLORIDA & The Keys - Where and how to plan a vacation to America's most popular fishing and diving destination. Features include artificial reef loran numbers; freshwater springs/caves; coral reefs/barrier islands; gulf stream/passes; inshore flats/channels; and back country estuaries.

BEST BOOK CONTENT!
"Fish & Dive the Caribbean" was a finalist in the Best Book Content Category of the National Association of Independent Publishers (NAIP). Over 500 books were submitted by publishers including Simon & Schuster and Turner Publishing. Said the judges "An excellent source book with invaluable instructions. Written by two nationally-known experts who, indeed, know what vacationing can be!"

DIVING SERIES by M. Timothy O'Keefe

(DL1) DIVING TO ADVENTURE shows how to get started in underwater photography, how to use current to your advantage, how to avoid seasickness, how to dive safely after dark, and how to plan a dive vacation, including live-aboard diving.

(DL2) MANATEES - OUR VANISHING MERMAIDS is an in-depth overview of nature's strangest-looking, gentlest animals. They're among America's most endangered mammals. The book covers where to see manatees while diving, why they may be living fossils, their unique life cycle, and much more.

UNCLE HOMER'S OUTDOOR CHUCKLE BOOK
by Homer Circle, Fishing Editor, Sports Afield

(OC1) In his inimitable humorous style, "Uncle Homer" relates jokes, tales, personal anecdotes and experiences covering several decades in the outdoors. These stories, memories and moments will bring grins, chuckles and deep down belly laughs as you wend your way through the folksy copy and cartoons. If you appreciate the lighter side of life, this book is a must!

OUTDOOR ADVENTURE LIBRARY
by Vin T. Sparano, Editor-in-Chief, Outdoor Life

(OA1) HUNTING DANGEROUS GAME - Live the adventure of hunting those dangerous animals that hunt back! Track a rogue elephant, survive a grizzly attack, and face a charging Cape buffalo. These classic tales will make you very nervous next time you're in the woods!

KEEP ME UPDATED!
"I would like to get on your mailing list. I really enjoy your books!"
G. Granger, Cypress, CA

(OA2) GAME BIRDS & GUN DOGS - A unique collection of tales about hunters, their dogs and the upland game and waterfowl they hunt. You will read about good gun dogs and heart-breaking dogs, but never about bad dogs, because there's no such animal.

COASTAL FISHING GUIDES
by Frank Sargeant

A unique "where-to" series of detailed secret spots for Florida's finest saltwater fishing. These guide books describe hundreds of little-known honeyholes and exactly how to fish them. Prime seasons, baits and lures, marinas and dozens of detailed maps of the prime spots are included. The comprehensive index helps the reader to further pinpoint productive areas and tactics. Over $160 worth of personally-marked NOAA charts in the two books.

(FG1) FRANK SARGEANT'S SECRET SPOTS Tampa Bay to Cedar Key
Covers Hillsborough River and Davis Island through the Manatee River, Mullet Key and the Suwannee River.

(FG2) FRANK SARGEANT'S SECRET SPOTS Southwest Florida
Covers from Sarasota Bay to Marco.

INSHORE SERIES
by Frank Sargeant

(IL1) THE SNOOK BOOK-"Must" reading for anyone who loves the pursuit of this unique sub-tropic species. Every aspect of how you can find and catch big snook is covered, in all seasons and all waters where snook are found.

(IL2) THE REDFISH BOOK-Packed with expertise from the nation's leading redfish anglers and guides, this book covers every aspect of finding and fooling giant reds. You'll learn secret techniques revealed for the first time. After reading this informative book, you'll catch more redfish on your next trip!

(IL3) THE TARPON BOOK-Find and catch the wily "silver king" along the Gulf Coast, north through the mid-Atlantic, and south along Central and South American coastlines. Numerous experts share their most productive techniques.

(IL4) THE TROUT BOOK -Jammed with tips from the nation's leading trout guides and light tackle anglers. For both the old salt and the rank amateur who pursue the spotted weakfish, or seatrout, throughout the coastal waters of the Gulf and Atlantic.

HUNTING LIBRARY
by John E. Phillips

(DH1) MASTERS' SECRETS OF DEER HUNTING - Increase your deer hunting success by learning from the masters of the sport. New information on tactics and strategies is included in this book, the most comprehensive of its kind.

(DH2) THE SCIENCE OF DEER HUNTING Covers why, where and when a deer moves and deer behavior. Find the answers to many of the toughest deer hunting problems a sportsman ever encounters!

(DH3) MASTERS' SECRETS OF BOW-HUNTING DEER - Learn the skills required to take more bucks with a bow, even during gun season. A must read for those who walk into the woods with a strong bow and a swift shaft.

(TH1) MASTERS' SECRETS OF TURKEY HUNTING - Masters of the sport have solved some of the most difficult problems you can encounter while hunting wily longbeards with bows, blackpowder guns and shotguns. Learn the 10 deadly sins of turkey hunting.

> **RECOMMENDATION!**
> *"Masters' Secrets of Turkey Hunting is one of the best books around. If you're looking for a good turkey book, buy it!"* J. Spencer, Stuttgart Daily Leader, AR
>
> **NO BRAGGIN'!**
> *"From anyone else Masters' Secrets of Deer Hunting would be bragging and unbelievable. But not with John Phillips, he's paid his dues!"* F. Snare, Brookville Star, OH

(BP1) BLACKPOWDER HUNTING SECRETS - Learn how to take more game during and after the season with black powder guns. If you've been hunting with black powder for years, this book will teach you better tactics to use throughout the year.

FISHING LIBRARY

(CF1) MASTERS' SECRETS OF CRAPPIE FISHING by John E. Phillips Learn how to make crappie start biting again once they have stopped, select the best jig color, find crappie in a cold front, through the ice, or in 100-degree heat. Unusual, productive crappie fishing techniques are included.

(CF2) CRAPPIE TACTICS by Larry Larsen - Whether you are a beginner or a seasoned crappie fisherman, this book will improve your catch! The book includes some basics for fun fishing, advanced techniques for year 'round crappie and tournament preparation.

> **CRAPPIE COUP!**
> *"After reading your crappie book, I'm ready to overthrow the 'crappie king' at my lakeside housing development!"* R. Knorr, Haines City, FL

(CF3) MASTERS' SECRETS OF CATFISHING by John E. Phillips is your best guide to catching the best-tasting, elusive cats. If you want to know the best time of the year, the most productive places and which states to fish in your pursuit of Mr. Whiskers, then this book is for you. Special features include how to find and take monster cats, what baits to use and when, how to find a tailrace groove and more strategies for rivers or lakes.

INDEX

CPSIA information can be obtained at www.ICGtesting.com
Printed in the USA
BVOW08s1715020215

386006BV00004B/11/P